In Your Best Interests

An empowering and protective system of guides and checklists that reduces your vulnerability to high-pressure sales tactics and self-serving "advice", while increasing your awareness and decision-making confidence when evaluating, selecting and working with financial advisors.

M. B. Robinson

Creator of the *Be a Money Smarty*™ system of guides and checklists
Author of *Your Money in the Balance*

In Your Best Interests

Disclaimer
The information, analysis and opinions (1) do not constitute professional investment, tax or legal advice; (2) are provided solely for educational purposes and therefore do not constitute an offer to buy or sell any security or pursue a specific investment strategy; (3) may not be suitable for every situation; (4) are not warranted or represented to be correct, complete or accurate.

There is no guarantee that by following *In Your Best Interests* you will: (1) achieve your investment goals; (2) generate investment profits or avoid losses; (3) avoid abusive or unscrupulous sales practices; (4) avoid unsuitable or inappropriate activity in your account; (5) avoid investment fraud. LifeGuide 360 and this publication's author cannot be held responsible for any of these occurrences.

The market returns and individual investment returns illustrated herein are hypothetical and do not represent actual returns.

The market indexes referenced are unmanaged and are composed of individual stocks and/or bonds. An investment cannot be made directly into an index.

Past performance is not indicative of future results. Future returns are not guaranteed and may differ substantially from historical returns. Future correlations between asset classes/investment categories and the future risk of any asset class/investment category or individual security may differ greatly from historical data. Diversification does not guarantee investment returns and does not eliminate the risk of significant loss.

Investing in stocks, bonds, mutual funds and ETFs involve considerable risks including the loss of principal. Stocks, bonds, mutual funds and exchange-traded funds (ETF) are not FDIC insured, offer no bank guarantee, may lose value, are not insured by any federal government agency and are not a deposit.

Prior to investing, consider your investment objectives and risk tolerance, understand the risks associated with each investment, and carefully read all prospectuses and equivalent disclosure statement(s).

This publication is not affiliated with any brokerage firm, insurance company, registered investment adviser, bank, credit union, mutual fund company, or any other type of financial services company, financial-related publication or service.

Note: "financial advisor" is used throughout this publication as a generic term for insurance agent, registered representative (broker), registered investment adviser (RIA), investment adviser rep (IAR) and non-legal terms such as investment executive, financial consultant, wealth manager and financial planner.

Table of Contents

Foreword

I bought my first investment in 1993 while I was a young Army officer stationed in Fort Sill, Oklahoma. I recall going to a financial advisor who presented me with two mutual fund options: a "growth" fund and a "value" fund. I couldn't make heads or tails of what the advisor was telling me. Afraid of asking "stupid" questions, I went ahead and invested $166.66 per month into a mutual fund based solely on my own interpretation of two words the advisor used: "growth" and "value". My thinking was this: I want my money to "grow" like crazy! So why would I want a fund that focused on the "value" of my money? What a smart young officer.

A couple of years later, I noticed that only 95 percent of my monthly investment was actually going into the mutual fund. My money wasn't growing like crazy, either. This was my first lesson in what I would later term "DKDK". You don't know what you don't know. And it's this imbalance between what you know, and what the "expert" financial advisor knows that places you at a great disadvantage when dealing with a highly-trained salesperson. How do you avoid the negative consequences of DKDK? Ask the right questions! A good question immediately shifts the power away from the salesperson to you.

After leaving the Army I became an investment adviser providing investment management services and retirement planning advice to hundreds of investing consumers. Over my 15-year career as an adviser I have held hundreds of client meetings. And in all these meetings, how many clients showed up with a note pad and took notes? Less than 10! This is not unusual. Most consumers only "show up" to their meeting with their financial advisor. They don't engage. They turn their brains on "listen only" and turn off "ask questions". In doing so, they place their interests at risk by passively capitulating to the "expert". This plays out thousands of times a day in financial services offices and conference rooms across America.

While there are highly-competent and credentialed financial advisors, there are also those who are less competent. Interestingly, some of the most competent financial advisors are terrible salespersons, while some of the least competent are world-class product pushers who lie in wait for the "leap of faith" customer.

Working with the wrong financial advisor can have unrecoverable, even life-altering consequences. What can you do? You have two choices: do the "leap of faith" thing, or ask questions that help you protect your money and your interests. What are the questions? They're here for you in *In Your Best Interests*.

With the *power of the question* you'll gain clarity, decision-making confidence, relief and peace.

Justin Michaels
Investor protection advocate, public speaker
February, 2015

4

Author's Note

The Power of Questions

In Your Best Interests was created from questions. Thousands of questions. They came from folks in rural farming communities in central and western Michigan, and from "Yoopers" in Marquette and the college town of Houghton. They came from residents of the Cherry Capital of the World, Furniture City, Motown, and the suburbs of southeastern Michigan. From 2007 to 2013 as part of Michigan's statewide investor education initiative, nearly 100,000 Michigan residents gathered at their local libraries and community centers to learn about investing and to ask questions. I had the privilege of developing content for the initiative, presenting it to the public, and listening to thousands of questions.

During this seven-year initiative I also spent hundreds of hours doing one-to-one counseling sessions with program attendees. This experience was remarkable for what it revealed. Very few asked questions about asset allocation, diversification or the markets. From large investor to small, from farmer to suburbanite, white color and blue, their questions were about their accounts and their financial advisor: "Does this look right?" "Can you explain this?" "I don't know what's going on." "What am I paying?" "How can I find out?" "I just want to know." "What do I ask?"

In all personal and professional relationships, when one side feels like they're in the dark and has questions, the other side needs to answer. "But I don't know what to ask" was commonly voiced. So without partiality or prejudice, I would help: "Go ask your advisor these questions exactly as I've written them." *In Your Best Interests* was taking form.

I encourage you to use this series of guides and checklists to bring openness, fair play and accountability to your initial and ongoing interactions with financial advisors. It's in your best interests!

M. B. Robinson
April 6, 2015

Getting Started

With every recommendation, consideration and action, the financial advisor who solicits you for business, or the financial advisor you're already working with, makes a conscious decision between two alternatives: 1) put your needs and interests first, or 2) put their own interests first at your expense. Rules and regulations do not guide their decision. It's guided by personal integrity, or by the absence of this trait.

Two Camps

Most financial advisors are guided by personal integrity. They put your needs and interests first. *In Your Best Interests* provides a way for you to confirm that your advisor is in this camp. Confirming this will naturally strengthen the relationship between you and your advisor as you gain further appreciation for the quality of care you receive.

In the other camp are those advisors who have a tendency to put their own interests first, often at your expense. What's worse, their salesmanship and social skills make it difficult to even know it's happening to you. You can't afford this kind of relationship. *In Your Best Interests* helps you protect your money and your interests by reducing your vulnerability to inexpert advisors, high-pressure sales tactics, self-serving "advice" and excessive costs.

Dear advisor: just a few questions...

The Power of Questions

Developed over a seven-year period with contributions from thousands of investing consumers, this ground-breaking system of guides and checklists:

☐ Helps you confirm that your financial advisor is putting your interests first, and is dealing with you openly, fairly, and with accountability.

☐ Helps alert you to a financial advisor who may be putting their own interests first, and may even be taking advantage of you.

☐ Helps you avoid the extreme risks to your money and future that can arise from high-pressure sales tactics, self-serving advice, "leap of faith" decisions and blind trust.

☐ Provides guidance on how to evaluate and select a financial advisor who's right for your needs, preferences and financial situation.

☐ May save you hundreds or even thousands of dollars every year by alerting you to excessive fees and commissions, hidden costs, or poor investment returns.

While brokerage/advisory firms provide disclosures and reports that communicate much of the information the *In Your Best Interests* checklists request,

☐ only your checklists promote and protect your interests with a set of questions from your side of the relationship,

☐ only your checklists equip you with questions that apply specifically to the decisions and actions of your financial advisor,

☐ only your checklists help you evaluate the intent of your financial advisor, and the quality and professionalism of your advisor, by how your questions are answered, and

☐ only your checklists allow you to record and file your financial advisor's direct responses to your questions.

Is This You?

How do you know which guide(s) to use? You can use the *Guides and Checklists Overview* section on page 8, or you can use *Is This You?* Developed from actual questions and comments noted by the author over a seven-year period (see *Author's Note*), this section contains 29 real-world situations and life events that either involve interaction with a financial advisor, or could prompt you into considering the services of one. When you find a situation that applies to you, just print the applicable guide and go!

My Best Interests Folder

To keep your checklists organized and together, create a *My Best Interests* folder to hold the checklists you complete with your financial advisor. Your folder will be a handy source for vital information about your account and provide historical documentation of your interactions with your advisor.

Retirement Plan Distribution Options   p. 16

When you leave your employer, you have basically three distribution options for your retirement account that avoid immediate taxes or possible tax penalties. To protect your money and your interests, use this guide before you make any decisions. The questionnaires and self-assessments will help you determine which distribution option is right for you.

Rolling Your Retirement Plan Account Into an IRA   p. 25

Financial institutions looking to "capture the rollover" spend tremendous amounts of money on advertising urging you to roll your account into an IRA. But don't be too quick to roll. It may not be in your best interests, regardless of what the advertisements may suggest. News Flash: When a financial advisor recommends a rollover of your retirement plan account into an IRA, *the recommendation must be suitable for you.* Use this guide to protect your money, your interests and your future. You can't afford to make a wrong and potentially unrecoverable decision with this vitally-important account.

☐ Checklist: *To Roll or Not to Roll*

This checklist provides a way for your financial advisor to explain why rolling your account into an IRA is suitable for you. It also asks your advisor to disclose his or her plans for investing your money, what the cost to do that might be, and the types of investments that may be used in the management of your account.

Buying an Annuity: Know What You're Buying and Why   p. 34

While annuities can provide valuable features and benefits under the right set of financial circumstances, they can also be wildly inappropriate under another set of circumstances. For most of us, annuities are confusing and difficult to understand. Unfortunately, there are unethical financial advisors who take advantage of this fact.

Checklists:

☐ *Fixed Annuities*
☐ *Indexed Annuities*
☐ *Variable Annuities*

Each *Annuity* checklist asks your advisor to justify *why* the annuity is right for you, and explain the features, benefits and costs associated with it. Using the checklists may also help you avoid getting stuck with the wrong annuity.

Buying a Mutual Fund: Know What You're Buying and Why   p.47

Don't get "sold" your next mutual fund. "Buy" the fund because you know it's right for you.

☐ Checklist: *Mutual Fund*

This checklist provides a way for your financial advisor to summarize important information about the mutual fund, and explain why it's right for you.

Financial Advisors: An Overview   p. 54

What's the difference between an agent, a registered representative and a registered investment adviser? Most investors don't know. This guide unlocks the mystery surrounding financial advisors by providing an overview of the three most popular types of advisors, the products and services they provide, how they are compensated, and the "standard of care" they are held to in the handling of client/customer accounts. Which type of advisor right for you? This guide will help you decide.

Your Financial Advisor: Finding Mr. or Ms. "Right" p. 61

Your relationship with a financial advisor can be one of your most important and valuable professional relationships. The nature of the relationship, the intent of your advisor, and the measurable competency of your advisor can have a tremendous impact on your financial well-being. You can't afford to get into the wrong relationship.

☐ Checklist: *Finding Mr. or Ms. "Right"*

Know who you're working with! This two-part checklist will help you find the right advisor for your financial situation, needs and preferences.

Your Financial Advisor: Is the Relationship Right? p. 76

Some of the attributes of a good business relationship with a financial advisor include skillful investment management, sound guidance and advice, a commitment to placing your interests first, good communication, and quality customer service. For many, an alignment of values is also important. When some of these attributes are lacking, it may lead to dissatisfaction. If you find that shortfalls or gaps exist between what your needs are and what your advisor is capable of providing, this guide provides direction on what to do.

☐ Checklist: *Assessing the Relationship*

This checklist will help you confirm that your advisor puts you first in the relationship, and that he or she provides the services most appropriate for your financial situation, needs and preferences. You can't afford to stay in the wrong relationship.

Your New Investment Account: Okay, What's the Plan? p. 83

You need to know how your financial advisor plans to invest your account before you invest a penny. Waiting to be surprised isn't good business. Use this guide when you are opening a new account.

☐ Checklist: *My New Investment Account*

This checklist asks your advisor to explain how he or she plans to invest your money, what the costs might be, and the types of investments that may be used in your account.

Your Investments: Know What You Own and Why p. 89

To protect your best interests, you need to know more than who your accounts are with and how much is in them. You need to know what's *inside* your accounts. While having trust in your financial advisor is part of a good relationship, blind trust may place you at risk. It's good business to confirm that your advisor is handling your account appropriately.

☐ Checklist: *My Investments*

This 4-point checklist provides a conversational way for your advisor to explain your account's allocation, level of diversification, and the individual investments you own. It also provides a way for your advisor to show that you come first in the relationship. News Flash: there isn't anything about your investments that can't be explained in a few key phrases!

Trading Activity: Commission-based Accounts p. 97

Before any "buy" or "sell" can be transacted in your account, your financial advisor is required to get your approval. Your advisor is also required to have a "reasonable basis" for believing that the trade is suitable for you. "Suitable" is regulatory-speak for "right for you".

☐ Checklist: *Trading Activity*

This checklist creates awareness of the trading activity in your account, and provides a simple way for you and your advisor to confirm that all the buys and sells in your account were authorized by you, and are suitable for you. Completing the checklist also provides a way for your advisor to show that you come first in the relationship.

Account Returns: Know How You're Doing and Compared to What p. 102

Saying your account "did pretty well" or was "down just a little" is a very loose way of evaluating how your investments are doing. A better way is to have your financial advisor answer two important questions about your account: "how is it doing?" and "compared to what?" Not knowing the answer to this two-part question could be costing you hundreds or even thousands of dollars every year.

☐ Checklist: *My Account's Return*

This easy-to-use checklist provides a way for you to know whether the rate of return on your account was good, or not-so-good, when compared to a standard or "benchmark". With this information you can determine whether your advisor's decisions are adding or subtracting value.

Total Costs: Commission and Fee-based Accounts p. 109 or p. 114

You probably know what you pay for most goods and services, but do you really know what you're paying in commissions, fees and other costs? Excessive commissions, fees and other costs are money out of your pocket! This can add up to a lot of money over a several-year period. You could be paying out hundreds or even thousands of dollars every year that you'd scream about paying - if you knew.

Checklists:

☐ *Total Costs: Commission-based Accounts*
☐ *Total Costs: Fee-based Accounts*

The *Total Costs* checklists for commission and fee-based accounts asks your financial advisor to itemize what you're paying for, and how much that is. Note: Controlling costs is a good way for your advisor to show that you come first in the relationship.

Investment Scams and Fraud: Too Good to be True? p. 119

Most of us think we'd never fall victim to a scam, but we do. We're all potential victims. In this guide you'll learn the red flags of investment scams and fraud. A checklist of two phone calls will help you protect yourself from any investment opportunity that really is "too good to be true."

Is This You?
Guides and Checklists for Your Situation

Developed from actual questions and comments noted by the author over a seven-year period (see *Author's Note*), this section contains 29 real-world situations and life events that either involve interaction with a financial advisor, or could prompt you into considering the services of one. When you find a situation that applies to you, just print the guide and go!

☐ **Retirement Plan Distribution Options Guide**   p. 16 <u>and</u>

☐ **Rolling Your Retirement Plan Account Into an IRA**   p. 25

Leaving Employer: Retirement Plan Distribution Options

"My wife is leaving her employer for employment elsewhere. We wonder what she should do with her 401(k) account. Do we leave it where it is? Do we roll it into her new employer's plan? Do we roll it over into an IRA? What do we need to consider that will help us make the right decision?"

Rollover My Retirement Plan Account into an IRA?

"With all the advertisements urging me to rollover my retirement account into an IRA, you'd think it's the only option I have. It also makes me wonder: is rolling into an IRA really the right thing for me to do? My financial advisor says it is, but is that enough to go on? This is my largest and most important account!"

Who vs. Where

"I'm being urged by a financial advisor to rollover my retirement account into an IRA with her company. Okay, it's a big company, but isn't having the right advisor more important than the company? Financial institutions are pretty much the same. Financial advisors aren't. How do I find one who will put my needs and interests first?"

Investment Options, Costs and the Value of Advice

"I'm satisfied with the investment options in my retirement plan, and the expenses are pretty low. But are there other things I should consider besides investment options and costs? What about advice on other important financial matters? Would rolling my account into an IRA with the right financial advisor be worth the additional costs? What can I use to help me make a more informed and beneficial decision?"

Trust

"My former co-worker's financial advisor would like me to rollover my retirement account into an IRA. But it's all about trust for me. The fact that my co-coworker likes him isn't enough. Familiarity doesn't mean trustworthy! There are too many headlines about so-called 'advisors' taking advantage of retirees. Laws and regulations to prevent this aren't enough for me. I want a way to confirm that the financial advisor is worthy of my trust."

☐ Buying an Annuity: Know What You're Buying and Why p. 34

Buy an Annuity?

"I don't know a lot about annuities, so how would I know if one is even right for me? A good sales pitch can make any annuity sound great. I worry that I could get steamrolled into buying! I'd like to have a way for the financial advisor to confirm that the annuity is right for me, and why. That would make me a lot more comfortable with the annuity – and with the advisor who's recommending it."

☐ Buying a Mutual Fund: Know What You're Buying and Why p. 47

Buy a Mutual Fund?

"A financial advisor is recommending that I buy a mutual fund. Okay, but I don't want to be sold a fund without first knowing why it's right for me. How can I look out for my interests?"

Buy Another Mutual Fund?

"My financial advisor is recommending that I buy another mutual fund. I don't want to buy another fund for the sake of buying another fund. I want to know how it fits in with the other funds I already have. And what about costs? How do I get an explanation?"

What About the Small or First-time Investor?

"My daughter and son-in-law are being solicited to take some of their savings and buy a mutual fund. This is a big move for them, and as a parent, I worry. How can they confirm - as newbies - that the mutual fund meets their needs, not just a financial advisor's sales quota?"

☐ Financial Advisors: An Overview p. 54

Evaluating a Financial Advisor

"I'd like to find a financial advisor to work with. But like most people, I don't know the difference between an agent, a broker, an investment executive, a wealth manager, a registered investment adviser and a financial planner. It's all very confusing. How do I find one who's right for me?"

☐ Your Financial Advisor: Finding Mr. or Ms. "Right" p. 61

Background on a financial Advisor

"I'd like more information on the financial advisor who's soliciting me. He'd like me to transfer my account from my current advisor over to him. How can I find whether he's really right for me? And how can I find out if he's been disciplined by regulators or has customer complaints against him?"

More Than Managing My Money

"Having a financial advisor to manage my investments is important, but I have other financial issues that are just as important to me. How do I find an advisor who can provide the kind of advice I need?"

Divorced and Starting Over

"I'm ready to hit the reset button and start over. I want to set new goals, and find a financial advisor who'll put my needs and interests first and invest my money in a way that's right for my new circumstances. How do I get started?"

Death of a Spouse: Now What?

"My husband recently passed away. He handled all our accounts and liked trading stocks through his financial advisor. Now I find out that my husband's advisor is automatically my advisor! I question whether he's even right for me. I'm not comfortable trading stocks, and our personalities don't mix well. What do I do?"

☐ Your Financial Advisor: Is the Relationship Right? p. 76

We Don't Talk About It

"I know about the risks of the stock market. Who doesn't? But longevity risk, lifestyle risk, funding risk? My financial advisor doesn't talk to me about these risks. I wonder if he could even advise me on them. Maybe it's because they require analysis and planning instead of a quick sale? I think I may have outgrown my advisor."

Unhappy with Financial Advisor

"I'm unhappy with the customer service I get from my financial advisor. She seems too busy for me. She's slow to return my calls, and when we do talk, I feel like I'm being rushed off the phone. Her assistant's work is a little sloppy, too! I'd like to give her a chance to resolve these problems, but if it doesn't work out, what do I do?"

Nice Person, Wrong Advisor for Me

"When it comes to the stock market, my financial guy sounds like he knows what he's talking about. But what worries me is that the stock market is all he wants to talk about. I don't need the latest buzz on the market. I can Google that! And I'm not sure the big talk shows up as big numbers on my account statement, either. This isn't working!"

Trust in Question

"I've trusted my financial advisor to do what's right for me, but I think I've been taken advantage of. While the investments he sold me weren't really wrong for me, I don't think they were really right for me, either. I think his interests were always placed ahead of mine."

Questioning my Questions

"My financial advisor makes me feel uncomfortable when I ask questions about the handling of my account. I guess she thinks the statements and reports I get are enough. I'm not questioning her, I just have questions. If one side of a relationship has questions, shouldn't the other side provide answers?"

☐ Your New Investment Account: Okay, What's the Plan?   p. 83

Shouldn't We Talk About This, First?

"I like surprises, but not when it comes to my money. When I open a new account, or add more money to my account, shouldn't I know beforehand what my financial advisor plans to do, and what types of investments might be used? A few key questions would be helpful."

☐ Your Investments: Know What You Own and Why   p. 89

How is Your Account Allocated? Do You Know?

"I know a little bit about asset allocation and how important it is, but I'm not really sure how my brokerage account is allocated. I take it on blind trust that I have the right allocation, but is this being smart? Is there a way for my financial advisor to confirm that my asset allocation is right for me? That's all I really want to know."

How is Your Account Diversified? Do You Know?

"I take it on blind trust that my financial advisor has my brokerage account diversified in a way that's right for me. But shouldn't I have an easy way to confirm that it is? I'm not questioning my advisor's professionalism, I just want to know. What questions do I ask?"

Do You Know What Investments You Own and Why?

"I'm not very knowledgeable about investing and frankly, I don't want to be. I take it on blind trust that that the investments in my account are right for me. But the fact that I know nothing about my investments gets me worried. Is there a way for my financial advisor to confirm that the investments in my account are right for me without getting into a lot of heavy explanations?"

☐ Trading Activity: Commission-based Accounts   p. 97

Trading Activity in Your Account: Too Hot or Not?

"My financial advisor regularly buys and sells investments in my account. I'm not questioning my advisor, but I'd like to have a way for him to confirm that the trading activity in my account is appropriate for me. It would go a long way in showing that he values our relationship and isn't taking advantage of me."

Elderly Parents: Not on Top of Things?

"My parents are getting older and I question whether they're really on top of what's going on in their investment accounts. There seems to be a lot of trading activity in their accounts. They are very trusting, and I worry that they are being taken advantage of. I'd like a way to confirm that everything is on the up-and-up."

☐ Account Returns: Know How You're Doing and Compared to What p. 102

Do You Know the Return on Your Account?

"My wife and I have no idea what our account has returned over the past few years. Are we getting anywhere? When we ask how our account is doing, we get answers like 'just fine' or 'don't worry about it'. We don't think we should settle for answers like that. We'd like to know the rate of return on our account, and whether that return is competitive. How do we get that information?"

☐ Total Costs: Commission or Fee-based Accounts p. 109 or p. 114

What Am I Really Paying?

"My husband and I know what we pay for most goods and services, but when it comes to our investment accounts, we really don't know. We've never asked, and we've never been told. That's not good business. We also wonder if there are other expenses we don't know about – and should. How do we find out what's really coming out of our pocket?"

☐ Investment Scams and Fraud: Too Good to be True? p. 119

Is This a Scam or a Slam Dunk?

"My friends and I have been approached by another member of our association to buy into an investment opportunity that guarantees a great return without any risk. We're told several other members are investing, so we're being urged to act now before it's sold out. I'm a little skeptical, but one member says he's too savvy to get scammed. He says the investment opportunity is a slam dunk! Okay, but it still sounds too good to be true."

Elderly Parents: Are Yours Vulnerable?

"My parents get a lot of unsolicited calls from salespersons. I wonder what's being pitched to them. Is it even legitimate? They are very trusting and not very street smart. I worry that they may be vulnerable to scam artists. Is there a way to quickly check out the salesperson and the investment opportunity they're pitching?"

Retirement Plan Distribution Options

To Avoid Immediate Taxes and Possible Penalties

When to Use

- ☐ When you are evaluating your retirement plan distribution options,

- ☐ When you're being solicited to rollover your retirement account into an IRA with a financial advisor you <u>are not</u> already working with, or

- ☐ When you're considering rolling your retirement plan account into an IRA with an advisor you <u>are</u> already working with.

  DON'T MAKE A SNAP DECISION. KNOW YOUR OPTIONS

Important Notes

- ☐ If a financial advisor is recommending a rollover of your retirement account into an IRA, and you <u>are not</u> already working with the advisor, use the following two guides <u>first:</u> (See Table of Contents)

    - ☐ Guide: *Financial Advisors: An Overview* p. 54

    - ☐ Guide: *Financial Advisors: Finding Mr. or Ms. "Right"* p. 61
      Checklist: *Finding Mr. or Ms. "Right",* Part 1 & Part 2 p. 64 and p. 73

- ☐ If you <u>are</u> already working with the advisor who is recommending a rollover of your retirement account into an IRA, use the following guide <u>first:</u>

    - ☐ Guide: *Your Financial Advisor: Is the Relationship Right?*
      Checklist: *Assessing the Relationship*

  KNOW WHO YOU'RE WORKING WITH. YOU CAN'T AFFORD TO GET INTO - OR STAY IN - THE WRONG RELATIONSHIP

Retirement Plan Distribution Options
To avoid immediate taxes and possible penalties

What to Know
When you leave your current employer, you have a number of distribution options for your retirement account. To avoid immediate taxes or possible tax penalties, there are basically three options available to you:

☐ Option 1: Keep your retirement plan account with your employer.

☐ Option 2: Rollover/transfer your retirement plan account to your new employer's retirement plan, if you're leaving your current employer for employment elsewhere.

☐ Option 3: Roll it over into an IRA.

Let's look at each option:

Option 1:
Keep your retirement plan account with your employer
Most retirement plans allow you to keep your account in the plan if it is above a certain amount. Check with your benefits department or your plan provider to see if your account balance qualifies. Typically, you'll continue to have access to all of the plan's resources and functionality.

Keeping your retirement plan account is easy; you don't have to do much of anything. But while doing 'what's easy' shouldn't be the primary consideration, there are potential advantages to keeping your retirement account with your employer. For example:

☐ **Low Fees**
The investment options in retirement plans generally have lower expenses than their identical retail versions. This is especially true for larger retirement plans.

" How do I know what I'm paying?"

> *" Your retirement plan account statement shows the dollar amount of the plan-related fees and expenses (whether "administrative" or "individual") actually charged to or deducted from your account, along with a description of the services for which the charge or deduction was made.*
>
> *It also shows the total annual operating expenses expressed as both a percentage of assets and as a dollar amount for each $1,000 invested. This information is important when comparing the costs of your retirement plan account against the costs of an IRA."*

☐ **Care and Due-diligence**
Retirement plans follow a rigorous set of criteria to select investment options that are appropriate for the plan. They use the same care and due diligence to ensure that the investment options continue to meet the criteria for inclusion in the plan. This level of care reduces the probability of having investment options in the plan that continually underperform their respective benchmarks or drift away from their stated investment category and investment objective.

17

☐ **Loans**
Retirement plans generally allow participants to take a loan under certain circumstances.

☐ **Penalty-free withdrawals**
Unlike an IRA, if you have not reached 59½, penalty-free withdrawals may be available from your work retirement plan under certain circumstances.

☐ **Required minimum distributions (RMD)**
In an IRA, you're required to take minimum distributions or RMDs from your account at age 70½. However, if you are still working at age 70½ and you continue to contribute to your work retirement account, RMDs may not apply.

☐ **Protection from creditors and legal judgments**
As a general matter, employer-sponsored accounts may offer greater protection from creditors, judgments, and the IRS. Laws vary from state to state. If this is a concern for you, seek qualified tax and legal advice.

Examples like these may provide a justification for leaving a portion or all of your retirement plan assets within your employer's plan. It's a good idea to seek qualified tax and legal advice before you decide.

" I'm satisfied with the investment options in my retirement plan, and the expenses are pretty low. But are there other things I should consider besides investment options and costs?"

" If you seek financial-related services beyond investment management, or you prefer to have a financial advisor manage you investments, you may want to consider Option 3: Rollover Your Retirement Plan Account into a Qualified IRA."

Option 2:
Transfer your retirement plan account to your new employer's retirement plan

If you are leaving your current employer for employment elsewhere, you may have the option to transfer your retirement plan into your new employer's retirement plan. To help you decide whether that's the right option for you, use the following questionnaire as a starting point:

Do you prefer the investment options in your current plan over those in your new employer's plan?

☐ Yes ☐ No ☐ No opinion

Are the fees and expenses associated with your new employer's plan higher, lower or about the same as those in your current plan?

☐ Higher ☐ Lower ☐ About the same

Does your current retirement plan offer better or more comprehensive educational resources and planning tools than does your new employer's plan?

☐ Yes ☐ No ☐ No opinion

If you use an independent fee-based investment advisory service to manage your retirement plan account, is a similar service available in your new employer's plan?

☐ Yes   ☐ No   ☐ Not applicable

Reviewing Your Answers

If you prefer the investment options in your current plan, if your current plan's fees and expenses are lower than those in your new employer's plan, and if the educational resources and planning tools are acceptable to you, then keeping your retirement account with your current employer may be an appropriate option for you. If you use an independent fee-based advisory service to manage your account, and your new employer's plan doesn't provide this service, then keeping your account with your current employer may be the appropriate option for you.

Conversely, if your new employer's plan offers a more diverse line-up of investment options, the expenses are comparable to those in your current plan, and if the educational and planning tools are acceptable to you, then rolling/transferring your retirement plan to your new employer's plan may be an appropriate option for you.

Other Things to Consider

Another potential benefit to consider in rolling/transferring your retirement plan over into your new employer's plan is that under certain conditions, you may be able to defer required minimum distributions if you're still working at your new place of employment after you turn age 70½. A potential downside for rolling your retirement plan into an IRA is that the minimum age for taking penalty-free withdrawals is 59½ instead of 55 with a retirement plan.

If you, or if you and your spouse have other investment accounts, another way to consider your options is how the retirement plan account fits in with your other accounts. For example, which plan offers features or benefits more to your liking, or offers unique investment options that aren't available in your other accounts.

Another consideration on deciding whether to transfer your retirement plan to your new employer's plan are your investment preferences. If you prefer more flexibility, or the ability to pursue investment strategies typically not available through an employer-sponsored retirement plan, then the next option, rolling your retirement plan into a qualified IRA, may be an appropriate option for you.

While most employers allow new employees to transfer-in their retirement plan account from their previous employer, they may impose a waiting period before you can transfer, so it's important to confirm with your new employer what the terms and conditions are for transferring-in your retirement plan account.

Note: If you are leaving your employer and are not immediately seeking new employment, and you plan on rolling your retirement plan into an IRA (Option 3), you may want to consider opening a separate IRA specifically for your retirement plan rollover and not commingle it with contributory IRAs. Seek advice from a tax professional before making a decision.

Option 3
Rollover your retirement plan account into an IRA

Financial institutions offering IRAs include banks and credit unions, insurance companies, mutual fund companies, discount and full-service brokerage firms and registered investment advisers. IRAs are also typically available through your employer's retirement plan provider.

Are there potential advantages to rolling your retirement plan into an IRA? Yes there are:

☐ **More Investment Options**
A self-directed IRA may provide access to investment options not generally available in a retirement plan. For example, individual stocks, individual bonds, exchange traded funds (ETF), alternative and non-traditional investments, and depending of the financial institution, access to initial public offerings (IPO).

☐ **More Investment Strategies**
IRAs may also allow you to pursue more specific or targeted investment strategies, including certain options strategies, and may provide unique or non-traditional diversification opportunities that are not generally available in a retirement plan.

☐ **Access to Additional Services**
Another potential advantage is the ability to work with a financial advisor who can provide other important financial-related services beyond investment management.

☐ **Beneficiary Flexibility**
IRAs also provide more flexibility in naming beneficiaries. If you are married, the beneficiary of your retirement plan account by law must be your spouse unless you obtain a signed release. In certain circumstances, having the flexibility to name beneficiaries other than your spouse for your IRA may be beneficial. Examples like these may provide a justification for rolling a portion, or all of your retirement plan account into an IRA.

But not so fast. Don't be too quick to be sold on the notion that the grass is greener on the other side. There are also potential disadvantages to rolling your retirement plan into an IRA:

☐ **Higher Expenses**
Total expenses in an IRA can be significantly higher than those in your retirement plan, especially if you're with a large retirement plan. One to two percentage points higher is not uncommon. This can add-up to thousands of dollars a year. Cross your fingers that the returns on your IRA always make up for the higher expenses you may be paying.

☐ **Level of Care and Due-diligence**
Retirement plans follow a rigorous set of criteria to select investment options that are appropriate for the plan. They are regarded as "prudent experts". Cross your fingers that your IRA is managed at this same level of care, knowledge and skill.

☐ **No Loans**
Unlike retirement plans, under no circumstances can you take a loan from an IRA.

☐ **Higher Minimum Age Requirement for Penalty-free withdrawals**
If you have not reached 59½, penalty-free withdrawals may be available from your work retirement plan under certain circumstances. This is not available with an IRA.

☐ **Required Minimum Distributions (RMD) Mandatory at 70½**
If you are still working at age 70½ and you continue to contribute to your work retirement account, RMDs may not apply. In an IRA you're required to take minimum distributions or RMDs from your account at age 70½.

"Okay, I've decided to rollover my account into an IRA"

If you decide that rolling your retirement plan account into an IRA is the appropriate option for you, the first thing you need to do is decide who's going to manage your IRA. You have basically two options: Option 1: manage your IRA yourself, and Option 2: have a financial advisor manage it for you. Before you make a decision, take this self- assessment. Your responses will help you determine which option may be in your best interests:

1. Do you recognize the vital role your retirement plan account plays in providing income and/or growth potential during your retirement years?

   ☐ Yes ☐ No

2. The trustees/fiduciaries of your retirement plan act at the level of "prudent expert" in selecting and monitoring the investment options. Do you believe you have the knowledge and skills necessary to select and monitor appropriate investments for your IRA?

   ☐ Yes ☐ Not so sure

3. How comfortable would you be in making all the investment decisions in your IRA and being solely responsible for the consequences of your decisions?

   ☐ Comfortable ☐ Not so comfortable

4. How confident are you in your ability to manage your IRA into your eighties and nineties when typically our ability to handle numbers is greatly diminished?

   ☐ Confident ☐ Not so confident

5. How would you react to a severe or extended downturn in the stock or bond market? Would you make knee-jerk decisions? Would you sell-out?

   ☐ No "knee-jerk" reactions ☐ Not so sure

6. How would you react to a significant run-up in the stock market? Would media hype and the fear of "missing out" overwhelm reasonable caution and pull you into assuming too much risk?

   ☐ Maintain reasonable caution ☐ Not so sure

7. Do you anticipate the need for other financial-related services offered through financial advisors?

   ☐ Yes ☐ No ☐ Not sure

Reviewing your Self-Assessment

If after completing and evaluating your answers to the self- assessment you decide to be a "do-it-yourselfer" and manage your IRA yourself, go to Option 1 on the next page.

If after completing the self- assessment you decide that it may be in your best interests to have a financial advisor manage your IRA for you, skip ahead to Option 2.

Option 1: Manage my IRA myself

If you decide to manage your IRA yourself, the following guides as examples of industry "best practices" for financial advisors. As a "do-it-yourselfer", use the guide's checklists on yourself to confirm that you're adding value and acting in your best interests. The guides have easy-to-follow instructions, and each checklist takes only a few minutes to complete:

- ☐ Guide: *Your Investments* p. 89
- ☐ Guide: *Trading Activity* p. 97
- ☐ Guide: *Account Returns* p. 102
- ☐ Guide: *Total Costs* p. 109 or p. 114

Option 2: Have a financial advisor manage my IRA for me.

Your relationship with a financial advisor can be one of your most important and valuable professional relationships. The nature of the relationship and the measurable competency of your advisor can have a tremendous impact on your financial well-being over what may be a multiple-decade relationship. Regardless of whether the relationship only involves your investments, or is broader in scope and more complex, *your* needs and *your* interests must come first. How does an advisor show that you come first? It's simple: three attributes need to be present. These attributes are intuitive, and apply to any important personal or professional relationship:

- ☐ Openness
- ☐ Fair Play
- ☐ Accountability

When this combination of inter-relationship decency and business ethics is present, a fourth attribute of a quality relationship shows up:

- ☐ Trust

Let's look at two scenarios:

Scenario 1
You're not yet working with a financial advisor.

When forming any new relationship, whether personal or professional, it's important to get to know the other person. This is especially true when it comes to selecting a financial advisor to handle what may be your largest and most important account. Use the following three-step process <u>before</u> you select an advisor and <u>before</u> you rollover your retirement account into an IRA:

Step 1
Use the following guide to familiarize yourself with the three basic types of advisors, the products and services they offer, and the standard of care they are held to in the handling of their clients' accounts:

- ☐ Guide: *Financial Advisors: An Overview* p. 54

Step 2
Use the following guide:

- ☐ Guide: *Financial Advisors: Finding Mr. or Ms. "Right"* p. 61
  Checklist: *Finding Mr. or Ms. "Right"*, Part 1 and Part 2 p. 64 and p. 73

Complete Part 1 of the checklist yourself. Part 1 will help you assess your needs and preferences, and help you decide which type of financial advisor may be appropriate for you. You'll then use Part 2 of the checklist when interviewing financial advisors. Bring your completed Part 1 to the meeting. It will serve as a handy reference for you and the advisor. Easy-to-follow instructions are in the guide.

Step 3
Before You Rollover a Penny...

If the financial advisor is recommending a rollover of your retirement account into an IRA, use the following guide:

- [ ] Guide: *Rolling Over Your Retirement Plan Account into an IRA* p. 25
  Checklist: *To Roll or Not to Roll* p. 31

The advisor provides all the answers the questions in the checklist. Only after reviewing the completed checklist with the advisor can you determine whether rolling over your retirement plan account into an IRA is right for you. Easy-to-follow instructions are in the guide.

Scenario 2:
You have an established relationship with a financial advisor

While your financial advisor may have been right for your needs and interests prior to retirement, is he or she the right advisor to manage your vitally-important retirement account? Ask yourself these questions about your advisor. How you answer may help you determine whether your current advisor is right for you going forward:

Is the relationship between you and your advisor based upon openness, fair play and accountability?

☐ Yes ☐ No ☐ Not sure

Do you come first in the relationship?

☐ Yes ☐ No ☐ Not sure

Does your advisor have the credentials, experience and expertise to handle what may be your largest and most important account?

☐ Yes ☐ No ☐ Not sure

Has your advisor added measurable value to the accounts you already have with them?

☐ Yes ☐ No ☐ Not sure

Are the total costs associated with the management of your account(s) disclosed?

☐ Yes ☐ No ☐ Not sure

Does your advisor offer other important financial-related services you anticipate needing?

☐ Yes ☐ No ☐ Not sure

In providing those services, would he or she be acting as an expert?

☐ Yes ☐ No ☐ Not sure

Step 1

To help you determine whether your current advisor continues to be Mr. or Ms. "Right" in light of your current financial situation, needs and preferences, use the following guide:

☐ Guide: *Your Financial Advisor: Is the Relationship Right?* p. 76
Checklist: *Assessing the Relationship* (completed by you) p. 80

Easy-to-follow instructions are in the guide.

Step 2

Your retirement plan account may be your largest and most important account. You can't afford to rollover this vitally-important account to a financial advisor who hasn't added measurable value, or acted in your best interests. You need to confirm two important things about your advisor:

1. That your advisor's management skills and cost-containment efforts have added measurable value to the account(s) you already have with him or her.

2. That he or she been acting in your best interests.

Use the following guides with your advisor to confirm that he or she has earned the privilege to handle your retirement account.

If your current accounts with your advisor are fee-based, use:

☐ Guide: *Account Returns* p. 102
☐ Guide: *Total Costs: Fee-based Accounts* p. 114

If your current accounts with your advisor are commission-based, use:

☐ Guide: *Account Returns* p. 102
☐ Guide: *Trading Activity* p. 97
☐ Guide: *Total Costs: Commission-based Accounts* p. 109

Your financial advisor provides all the information to complete the checklists. Reviewing them with your advisor takes only a few minutes. Easy-to-follow instructions are in the guides.

Step 3

Before You Rollover a Penny...

If you are considering rolling your retirement account into an IRA with your current advisor, use the following guide:

☐ Guide: *Rolling Over Your Retirement Plan Account into an IRA* p. 25
Checklist: *To Roll or Not to Roll* p. 31

Your advisor provides all the answers to the questions in the checklist. Only after reviewing the completed checklist with your advisor can you determine whether rolling your retirement plan account into an IRA is right for you. Easy-to-follow instructions are in the guide.

Rolling Over Your Retirement Plan Account

Is Rolling Your Account Into an IRA the Right Thing to Do?

Checklist

To Roll or Not to Roll p. 31

How Long Does it Take to Do?

About 30 minutes. Your financial advisor provides all the information.

When to Use

☐ Use when you're being solicited by a financial advisor to rollover your retirement plan account into an IRA. The checklist provides a way for the advisor to itemize *why* rolling your retirement account into an IRA is the right thing to do.

YOU CAN'T AFFORD TO MAKE A WRONG AND POTENTIALLY UNRECOVERABLE DECISION

Applies To

☐ Full-service advisors affiliated with your retirement plan provider

☐ Full-service advisors at brokerage firms, banks and credit unions

☐ Advisors at Registered Investment Adviser (RIA) firms

☐ Insurance agents

Important Notes

☐ Read the *Retirement Plan Distribution Options* guide <u>before</u> you use this guide.

☐ If you <u>are not</u> already working with the financial advisor who is recommending a rollover of your account into an IRA, use the following two guides <u>first</u>:

> ☐ Guide: *Financial Advisors: An Overview* p. 54

> ☐ Guide: *Financial Advisors: Finding Mr. or Ms. "Right"* p. 61
> Checklist: *Finding Mr. or Ms. "Right"*, Part 1 & Part 2 p. 64 and p. 73

KNOW WHO YOU'RE WORKING WITH. YOU CAN'T AFFORD TO GET INTO THE WRONG RELATIONSHIP

☐ Photocopy the checklist before using.

Rolling Over Your Retirement Plan Account Into an IRA

Dear advisor: just a few questions...

Instructions

Using the checklist:

☐ READ THROUGH THE CHECKLIST INSTRUCTIONS BEFORE USING

☐ Use during a meeting or phone call with your financial advisor. Your advisor provides all the information to complete the checklist. You fill in the answers.

☐ For questions 1, 2, 3 and 10, have your advisor answer using key phrases.

☐ Repeat what you've written back to your advisor.

☐ Your advisor has a regulatory obligation to answer your questions to your level of satisfaction. You can't afford a fuzzy understanding of what's going on with your money!

What do I say to my advisor?

Using your own words, here's what you want to convey: *"To help me better understand why rolling my retirement account into an IRA is right for me, I'd appreciate it if you'd answer the questions I have on my checklist. Your willingness to do this goes a long way in showing me that I come first in our relationship, and that the trust and confidence I'm placing in you is well-founded."*

Notes:

☐ While your financial advisor will have account agreements, contracts and disclosures that communicate much of the information your checklist requests,

- only your checklists promote <u>and protect your interests</u> with a set of questions from <u>your side</u> of the relationship,

- only your checklists equip you with questions that <u>apply specifically</u> to the decisions and actions of your financial advisor,

- only your checklists help you evaluate the <u>intent</u> of your financial advisor, and the <u>quality and professionalism</u> of your advisor, by how your questions are answered,

- only your checklists allow you to <u>record and file</u> your financial advisor's direct responses to your questions.

☐ The checklist questions are based on industry "best practices" for disclosure. There are no "zinger" or "gotcha" questions.

☐ Beware of evasive answers or claims that it's "against company policy" to answer.

After completion:

☐ Review for accuracy and completeness with your financial advisor.

☐ File the completed checklist in your *My Best Interests* folder.

The Checklist
The Importance of the Questions

Let's go over the questions on the checklist:

1. **What is your basis for believing that rolling my work retirement account into an IRA is suitable for me?**

     Most of us expect our financial advisor to do what's right for us. "Doing what's right" is intuitive. We don't need legal definitions to know what it means and the intent behind it. But there is one regulatory term you need to know about: "suitability".

    "Suitability?"

    "Suitability" is regulatory-speak for "doing what's right". Your advisor has a <u>regulatory obligation</u> to only make recommendations that are suitable or "right" for your needs, financial situation, investment objective, risk tolerance, etc. <u>This includes recommending you to rollover your retirement plan account into an IRA</u>."

    ? Okay... So what does a good answer look like?

    A good answer provides <u>specific</u> explanations on *why* rolling your retirement plan account into an IRA is suitable for you. You want these explanations itemized in key phrases. Note: <u>Generalized explanations that could apply to anybody are not a good answer.</u> This is about what's right for you! The explanations must apply specifically to you, your financial situation, your needs, and your preferences. <u>The promise of higher returns is not a good answer, either.</u> Refer to the guide titled *Retirement Plan Distribution Options* for helpful information under Option 3.

2. **Will you put me first in our relationship, and not advance your interests or those of your company at my expense?**

     Question 1 is about satisfying the regulatory requirement of "suitability". <u>Question 2 is about satisfying you</u>. It sets the terms on how your relationship with your advisor is going to work.

    Note: With every recommendation and every action, your financial advisor makes a conscious decision to either put your interests first, or their own interests first. <u>News Flash: regulations and "standard of care" rules do not guide this decision.</u> It's guided by personal integrity, or by the absence of this trait.

    ? What does a good answer look like?

    A direct "yes" is the only acceptable answer. You can't afford to enter into a relationship with a financial advisor who won't put you first.

3. How do you plan on investing my account?

Waiting to be surprised on how your account is going to be invested isn't good business. Your retirement account may be your largest and most important account. You need to know how your financial advisor plans to invest your IRA before you transfer a penny.

? What does a good answer look like?

It doesn't need to be a complicated answer. All you're looking for is a brief explanation of what your advisor's strategy is for your account, and the types of investments he or she might consider using. That's it. Your advisor has a regulatory obligation to make sure you understand their answer.

Note: If your advisor is recommending an annuity, he or she must also complete the appropriate *Buying an Annuity* checklist before you make a decision. No excuses. Also, if your IRA is a commission-based account, and your IP is recommending mutual funds, he or she must also complete the *Buying a Mutual Fund* checklist for each fund being recommended. This does not apply to fee-based IRAs.

4. How does this differ from what I can do in my retirement plan account?

? What does a good answer look like?

A good answer may include the availability of certain types of investments that are not available in your retirement account, the ability to use highly-focused or theme-based strategies, and guaranteed income strategies. A few key phrases that you understand are all you need.

5. How will you receive compensation for the handling of my account?

Depending on whether your account is commission-based, fee-based or fee-only, your advisor can receive compensation in different ways. For example, if your account is commission-based, your advisor may receive compensation from items "A" through "E" (see checklist on page 31). If your advisor is also licensed to sell insurance products, he or she may also receive compensation for item "F". If your account is fee-based, your advisor will typically receive item "G" compensation. If your advisor is also licensed to sell insurance products, he or she may also receive compensation through item "F".

? What does a good answer look like?

You expect your advisor to disclose all potential sources of compensation. Confirm with your advisor that all applicable boxes are checked. If your account is going to be fee-based or fee-only, you expect the applicable percentage (if the advisory fee is a percentage of the assets under management), hourly rate, or terms to be disclosed.

6. What is the estimated total cost to initially invest my account stated as a dollar amount and as a percentage of my expected opening account value?

If your advisor intends to open a commission-based account for your IRA, up-front sales charges and other costs can add up during the initial investing phase.

? What does a good answer look like?

Don't expect a to-the-penny accounting of these costs. All you're really looking for is a good faith estimate of what those initial costs may be. This is important because those costs can be avoided simply by keeping your retirement plan account where it is.

If your advisor plans on using a fee-based "managed" platform/program for your IRA, you want to know what the advisory fee will be and the payment terms. For example, a fee based upon the size of the account, an hourly rate, flat fee, etc.

7. **What is the estimated total cost to manage my account on an annual basis? Please state as a dollar amount range and as a percentage range based upon my expected opening account value.**

Your retirement plan statement also shows the total annual operating expenses of your investment options and shows those expenses as both a percentage of assets and as a dollar amount for each $1,000 invested. You should expect the same for your IRA.

? What does a good answer look like?

Both the dollar amount and percentage estimates are filled in. This range should also include any mutual fund/ETF internal expenses and mark-up/mark-downs associated with the management of your account. Refer to Quick Course: *Calculating Total Costs*, p. 133, for more information. Note: Having a good faith estimate of annual total costs will give you a straight-up comparison to the total costs you're paying in your retirement plan.

8. **Will you provide a performance report on my account that is measured against an appropriate benchmark at least annually?**

Your retirement plan provides investment performance on the investment options in the plan. Your plan also provides benchmark information on the investment options in the form of broad-based market index returns. Many retirement plans even provide individualized rates of return for plan participant accounts. If you do decide to rollover your retirement plan account into an IRA, it's in your best interests to make sure you'll receive a periodic report on your account is performing.

Note: If your account is with a commission-based broker, he or she can typically generate an "on demand" performance report on your account right from their computer. They may, however, be prohibited by company policy from calculating a benchmark return to compare your account's return against. If your advisor is prohibited from calculating a benchmark return, there's a workaround: you can do the calculations yourself. It only takes a few minutes, and the math is easy. Refer to Quick Courses: *Calculating Returns*, p. 127, and *Benchmarking Returns*, p. 129.

If your account is fee-based, you'll typically receive a report that includes your account's return compared against a benchmark. While this report provides valuable information, only your checklist promotes and protects your interests with a set of specific questions from your side of the relationship.

? Okay… So what does a good answer on performance reporting look like?

Your IP answered "yes". Note: Check out Quick Courses: *Calculating Returns*, p. 127, and *Benchmarking Returns*, p. 129.

9. **What other financial-related services do you provide? (Check all that apply)**

While investment options, fees and expenses are important considerations when deciding whether to rollover your retirement account, there are other considerations that may be equally important to you. For example, you may be interested in financial-related services that are not available through your retirement plan, and decide that having one-stop access to these services through a financial advisor may be worth any additional costs.

? What does a good answer look like?

You want to see boxes checked next to those services you may be interested in or anticipate needing. While most IPs provide these services for not additional charge, some IPs do charge a fee.

10. In providing these services, are you regarded as an expert?

? What does a good answer look like?

Your advisor answered "yes". Note: The fact that your advisor's brokerage/advisory firm offers other financial-related services doesn't mean your advisor is an expert in providing those services. Having an IP with specialized training and expertise may be important to you.

11. How does your client communication and ongoing educational/informational services compare to those offered through my retirement plan?

Your retirement plan offers many valuable tools and educational resources. While working with an advisor may remove the need for many of these resources, receiving educational and informative material from your financial advisor is still important.

? What does a good answer look like?

Many advisors offer educational workshops or seminars on investment-related topics to their clients and the community. This may be important to you.

Special Note: Your relationship with your financial advisor should be one of your most important and valuable professional relationships. Your checklist allows you to gauge the quality of this relationship by how your advisor answers your questions. Your checklist also allows you to confirm that your advisor puts you first, and that the relationship is based upon openness, fair play and accountability. You can't afford a relationship that doesn't work this way.

To Roll or Not to Roll

Date: _____

1. What is your basis for believing that rolling my retirement account into an IRA is suitable for me? Please answer using key phrases.

   _____

   _____

   _____

   _____

   _____

2. Will you put me first in our relationship and not advance your interests or those of your company at my expense?

   ☐ Yes ☐ No

3. How do you plan on investing my account?

   _____

   _____

   _____

   _____

   Types of investments you may consider using: (Check all that apply)

   ☐ Individual stocks, ETFs, etc.

   ☐ Individual bonds

   ☐ Mutual funds

   ☐ Annuities and other insurance-related products

   ☐ Fee-based "managed" account

   ☐ Other: _____

4. How does this differ from what I can do in my retirement plan account?

   _____

   _____

   _____

   _____

5. How will you receive compensation for handling my account? (Check all that may apply)

☐ A: Commissions from buying and selling of individual stocks, ETFs, etc.

☐ B: Mark-ups and mark-downs from buying and selling of individual bonds

☐ C: Commissions/up-front sales charges on the purchase of mutual funds

☐ D: Sales concessions from new securities offerings

☐ E: "Trailer"/service fees on mutual funds (typically between 0.25% and 1.00%)

☐ F: Commissions on the purchase of annuities and other insurance-related products

☐ G: Advisory fee as a percentage of assets under management: _____%

☐ H: Hourly rate for advisory services: Rate: $_____ an hour

☐ I: Retainer for advisory services: Terms: _____

☐ Other: _____

Notes: _____

_____

6. What is the estimated total cost to initially invest my account stated as a dollar amount and as a percentage of my expected opening account value?

$ _____ or _____ % of account value

7. What is the estimated total cost to manage my account on an annual basis? Please state as a dollar amount range and as a percentage range based upon my expected opening account value.

Between $ _____ and $ _____ / Between _____ % and _____ %

8. Will you provide a performance report on my account that is measured against an appropriate benchmark at least annually?

☐ Yes ☐ No

9. Do you provide services that are unavailable in my retirement plan? (Check all that apply)

☐ College planning

☐ Financial planning

☐ Insurance planning

☐ Tax-efficient investment strategies

☐ IRA/retirement plan withdrawal strategies

☐ Legacy and generational planning

☐ Special needs planning

☐ Post-divorce planning

☐ Other: _____

Are there additional costs for these services?

☐ Yes   ☐ No   If "Yes" $: _____

10. In providing these services, are you regarded as an expert?

☐ Yes   ☐ No

11. How does your client communication and ongoing education/informational services compare to those offered through my retirement plan

_____

_____

_____

_____

Buying an Annuity

Know What You're Buying and Why

Checklists

How Long Does it Take to Do?

About 25 minutes. Your financial advisor provides all the information.

When to Use

☐ Use this guide when an annuity is being recommended to you by a financial advisor. The checklists in this guide provide a way for your advisor to explain *why* the annuity is right for you.

KNOW WHAT YOU'RE BUYING, AND WHY. YOU CAN'T AFFORD GETTING STUCK WITH THE WRONG ANNUITY

Notes

☐ If you <u>are not</u> already working with the financial advisor who is recommending the annuity, use the following two guides <u>first:</u>

☐ Guide: *Financial Advisors: An Overview*   p. 54

☐ Guide: *Financial Advisors: Finding Mr. or Ms. "Right"*   p. 61
Checklist: *Finding Mr. or Ms. "Right",* Part 1 & Part 2   p. 64 and p. 73

KNOW WHO YOU'RE WORKING WITH. YOU CAN'T AFFORD TO GET INTO THE WRONG RELATIONSHIP

☐ Photocopy the checklist before using.

Buying an Annuity
Dear advisor: just a few questions...

Instructions

Using the checklist:

☐ If you are working with a financial advisor, the best way to complete the checklist is during a meeting with your advisor. Your advisor provides all the information to complete the checklist. You fill in the answers.

☐ If you are not working with the advisor who is recommending the annuity, you can mail or email the checklist to the advisor to complete and return to you. After you look over the answers, you can decide whether you want to move forward.

☐ Financial advisors have a regulatory obligation to answer your questions to your level of satisfaction. You can't afford a fuzzy understanding of what's going on with your money!

What do I say to my advisor?

Using your own words, here's what you want to convey: *"To help me better understand why the annuity you're recommending is right for me, I'd appreciate it if you'd complete my [fixed, indexed or variable] annuity checklist. Your willingness to do this goes a long way in showing me that I come first our relationship, and that the trust and confidence I'm placing in you is well-founded."*

Notes:

☐ While your financial advisor may provide you with annuity brochures and other documents that contain much of the information your checklist requests,

- only your checklists promote and protect your interests with a set of questions from your side of the relationship,

- only your checklists equip you with questions that apply specifically to the decisions and actions of your financial advisor,

- only your checklists help you evaluate the intent of your financial advisor, and the quality and professionalism of your advisor, by how your questions are answered,

- only your checklists allow you to record and file your financial advisor's direct responses to your questions.

☐ The checklist questions are based on industry "best practices" for disclosure. There are no "zinger" or "gotcha" questions.

☐ Beware of evasive answers or claims that it's "against company policy" to answer.

After completion:

☐ Review for accuracy and completeness with your financial advisor.

☐ File the completed checklist in your *My Best Interests* folder.

What to Know

Annuities are investment products developed by insurance companies. Annuities are generally considered to be longer-term investments. The general attributes and optional benefits of annuities may include: guarantee of principal (in fixed and indexed annuities), tax deferral, death benefits and income benefit riders that include lifetime income. Many annuities include long-term care benefits and/or a waiver of surrender charges if you become confined to a nursing facility. As a result, annuities typically carry higher overall expenses than do mutual funds. <u>One important distinction between annuities and most other investments is that they may impose a significant penalty for large withdrawals or for surrendering (cashing-out) the annuity contract before a certain date.</u>

Annuities are bought through a financial advisor/agent who has the proper licensing and registration to sell annuities. Most insurance companies require the financial advisor/agent to be trained and certified in order to sell their annuity products. With this training and certification, the advisor/agent recommending an annuity to you is considered to be an expert.

 This is the most important question on the checklist.

Most of us expect our financial advisor to do what's right for us. "Doing what's right" is intuitive. We don't need legal definitions to know what it means and the intent behind it. But there is one regulatory term you need to know about: "suitability".

❝ Suitability?"

> *❝ Suitability" is regulatory-speak for "doing what's right". It means your advisor has a regulatory obligation to only recommend an annuity that is suitable or "right" for your needs financial situation, investment objective, risk tolerance, etc."*

Going beyond the rules, if you don't understand the annuity, or it doesn't make sense to you, it probably isn't right for you.

Quick Course: Three Types of Annuities

In a **fixed-rate annuity**, the insurance company guarantees the contract holder a specific interest rate for a specified timeframe. Often 1 to 10 years. Fixed annuities are often used as an alternative to CDs and savings accounts. Note: Unlike <u>CDs and savings accounts, fixed annuities are not FDIC insured</u>. They are backed by the claims-paying ability of the insurance company. That's why the financial strength of the issuing insurance company is important.

An **indexed annuity** combines guarantees on your principal, a minimum guaranteed return, and/or the potential for a higher return that is "linked" to a selected market index. "Linking" means that the annuity monitors the index your contract is tied to and credits your contract when the index goes up, while not deducting from the value of contract when the index goes down.

A **variable annuity** allows you to invest in the stock and bond market through underlying mutual funds known as "sub-accounts" in the annuity. The value of the annuity is "variable" and dependent upon the performance of the underlying funds. Like other types of annuities, variable annuities offer several types of optional guarantees, benefits and income options.

What to Do

Before you buy an annuity, you need to complete the *My Annuity Due Diligence* checklist.

The second part of the process involves the financial advisor who is recommending the annuity. There are three checklists in this guide: one for fixed annuities, one for indexed annuities and one for variable annuities. Present the advisor with the checklist that corresponds with the type of annuity being recommended. Have them complete all the items on the checklist.

The checklist provides a handy way for the advisor to explain the annuity's features and benefits, the costs of the benefits or 'riders', other fees and expenses, the liquidity provisions and the surrender charges. It also provides a way for the advisor to explain *why* the annuity is suitable based upon your needs, investment objectives and overall financial situation. .

? How do I know if the annuity checklist is completed properly?

- ☐ Every box is checked
- ☐ Every field is filled
- ☐ All the answers have been explained to your level of satisfaction.

Note: Your financial advisor has a regulatory obligation to answer your questions to your level of satisfaction. You can't afford a fuzzy understanding of what's going on with your money! Remember, if you don't understand the annuity, or it doesn't make sense to you, it probably isn't right for you

Note: While your financial advisor may provide you with brochures and other documents that contain much of the information your checklist requests,

- ☐ only your checklist promotes and protects your interests with a set of specific questions from your side of the relationship,

- ☐ only your checklist allows you to record and file your financial advisor's direct responses to those questions,

- ☐ only your checklist equips you with questions that apply specifically to the decisions and actions of your financial advisor, and

- ☐ only your checklist helps you evaluate the intent of your financial advisor, and the quality and professionalism of your advisor, by how your questions are answered.

My Annuity Due Diligence

This checklist is the first of a two-part due diligence process for determining whether the annuity being recommended passes two levels of scrutiny: 1) your state's insurance regulators, and 2) yours.

This checklist is to be completed by you. Checking the boxes will confirm that the insurance company, the annuity, and the financial advisor recommending it are properly licensed and registered with the insurance regulatory authorities in your state.

Use this website to get contact information for your state's insurance regulator:
http://www.naic.org/state_web_map.htm

Contact your state's insurance regulators and confirm the following:

☐ The insurance company is registered and licensed with my state's insurance regulators.

Date: _____

☐ The insurance product being recommended is registered with my state's insurance regulators.

Date: _____

☐ The agent/broker recommending the annuity is registered with my state's insurance regulators and has the proper licenses to sell insurance products in my state.

Date: _____

Fixed Annuity

Dear advisor: just a few questions...

Date: _____

Instructions for the financial advisor:

Please provide the information requested for each check point. When you've completed the checklist, we can meet to have you explain each check point to me and to answer any questions I may have.

Financial Advisor: _____

Insurance Product: _____

1. Based upon my needs, investment objectives and overall financial situation, what specific features, benefits/riders of this annuity lead you to believe that this annuity is suitable for me?

   _____

   _____

   _____

   _____

2. Financial rating of issuing insurance company:

   Moody's: _____ (High-quality: Aaa, Aa; Medium: A, Baa; Speculative: Ba, B; Poor standing: Caa)

   S&P: _____ (Strong: AAA, AA, A; Adequate: BBB; Vulnerable: BB, B, CCC, CC, C)

   A.M. Best: _____ (Superior: A++, A; Excellent A, A-; Good: B++, B+; Fair B, B-; Marginal: C++, C+)

3. Initial rate being credited:

   Rate: _____

4. Is it a "bonus rate"?

   ☐ Yes ☐ No

   Bonus rate terms: _____

5. Does the bonus rate extend the surrender period?

   ☐ Yes ☐ No   If "Yes": From _____ years to _____ years

39

6. What is the guaranteed annualized minimum rate of return for over the length of the contract (entire surrender period)?

Guaranteed annualized minimum rate: _____%

7. How and when is the new rate is declared, and what are the terms?

Terms: _____

_____

8. Surrender Term (after which surrender charges do not apply):

Years: _____

9. Surrender charge by year (stated as a percentage and as a dollar amount of the original premium amount):

Yr 1: % ____ $_____   2: % ____ $_____   3: % ____ $_____

Yr 4: % ____ $_____   5: % ____ $_____   6: % ____ $_____

Yr 7: % ____ $_____   8: % ____ $_____   9: % ____ $_____

Yr 10: % ____ $_____   11: % ____ $_____   12: % ____ $_____

Yr 13: % ____ $_____   14: % ____ $_____   15: % ____ $_____

10. Are penalty-free withdrawals available during surrender period?

☐ Yes ☐ No

Terms/conditions: _____

_____

11. Is there a Long-term Care waiver or rider associated with the annuity?

☐ Yes ☐ No

Terms/conditions: _____

_____

12. Is there a wavier associated with terminal illness?

☐ Yes ☐ No

Terms/conditions: _____

_____

13. "Free look" period:

Period: _____

Indexed Annuity

Dear advisor: just a few questions...

Date: _____

Instructions for the financial advisor:

Please provide the information requested for each check point. When you've completed the checklist, we can meet to have you explain each check point to me and to answer any questions I may have.

Financial Advisor: _____

Insurance Product: _____

1. Based upon my needs, investment objectives and overall financial situation, what specific features, benefits/riders of this annuity lead you to believe that this annuity is suitable for me?

   _____
   _____
   _____
   _____

2. Financial rating of issuing insurance company:

   Moody's: _____ (High-quality: Aaa, Aa; Medium: A, Baa; Speculative: Ba, B; Poor standing: Caa)

   S&P: _____ (Strong: AAA, AA, A; Adequate: BBB; Vulnerable: BB, B, CCC, CC, C)

   A.M. Best: _____ (Superior: A++, A; Excellent A, A-; Good: B++, B+; Fair B, B-; Marginal: C++, C+)

3. "Floor" or guaranteed minimum interest rate:

   Rate: _____

4. Is there a guaranteed minimum contract value?

   ☐ Yes ☐ No

   Terms: _____
   _____

5. What market indices can the annuity be linked to?

   Index: _____ Index: _____

   Index: _____ Index: _____

6. Crediting Method:

☐ Annual reset ☐ High-water mark ☐ Point-to-point ☐ Month-to-Month

☐ Bi-Annual ☐ Other method

Explanation of method: _____

_____

7. Does a "Participation Rate" apply to the recommended Crediting Method?

☐ Yes ☐ No

Explanation: _____

_____

8. Does a "Cap Rate" apply to the recommended Crediting Method?

☐ Yes ☐ No

Explanation: _____

_____

9. Does a "Margin" or "Spread" apply to the recommended Crediting Method?

☐ Yes ☐ No

Explanation: _____

_____

10. What are the administrative expenses?

Itemize: _____

11. Surrender Period (after which surrender charges do not apply):

Years: _____

12. Surrender charge by year (stated as a percentage and as a dollar amount of the original premium amount.):

Yr 1: % ____ $_____   2: % ____ $_____   3: % ____ $_____

Yr 4: % ____ $_____   5: % ____ $_____   6: % ____ $_____

Yr 7: % ____ $_____   8: % ____ $_____   9: % ____ $_____

Yr 10: % ____ $_____   11: % ____ $_____   12: % ____ $_____

Yr 13: % ____ $_____   14: % ____ $_____   15: % ____ $_____

13. Are penalty-free withdrawals available during surrender period?

☐ Yes ☐ No

Terms/conditions: _____

_____

14. Is there a Long-term Care waiver or rider associated with the annuity?

☐ Yes ☐ No

Terms/conditions: _____

_____

15. Is there a wavier associated with terminal illness?

☐ Yes ☐ No

Terms/conditions: _____

_____

16. What optional riders or guarantees are available with this annuity?

Explain: _____

_____

_____

17. "Free look" period:

Period: _____

Variable Annuity

Date: _____

Instructions for the financial advisor:

Please provide the information requested for each check point. When you've completed the checklist, we can meet to have you explain each check point to me and to answer any questions I may have.

Financial Advisor: _____

Insurance Product: _____

1. Based upon my needs, investment objectives and overall financial situation, what specific features, benefits/riders of this annuity lead you to believe that this annuity is suitable for me?

    _____

    _____

    _____

    _____

2. Financial rating of issuing insurance company:

    Moody's: _____ (High-quality: Aaa, Aa; Medium: A, Baa; Speculative: Ba, B; Poor standing: Caa)

    S&P: _____ (Strong: AAA, AA, A; Adequate: BBB; Vulnerable: BB, B, CCC, CC, C)

    A.M. Best: _____ (Superior: A++, A+; Excellent A, A-; Good: B++, B+; Fair B, B-; Marginal: C++, C+)

3. Is it a "bonus credit" product?

    ☐ Yes ☐ No

    Bonus rate terms: _____

4. Does the bonus credit increase the internal expenses of the annuity?

    ☐ Yes ☐ No   If "Yes": From _____ % to _____ %

5. If the bonus credit does increase internal expenses, do these extra costs drop off after the surrender period?

    ☐ Yes ☐ No

4. Please list the fund/sub-account(s) you are recommending and its annual expenses:

Sub-account name: _____ Expense: _____%

Sub-account name: _____ Expense: _____%

Sub-account name: _____ Expense: _____%

Sub-account name: _____ Expense: _____%

Sub-account name: _____ Expense: _____%

Sub-account name: _____ Expense: _____%

5. Are the selected funds/sub-accounts suitable for me? ☐ Confirmed "yes"

6. How do you characterize the overall recommended sub-account investment plan you are recommending?

☐ Conservative   ☐ Moderate Conservative   ☐ Moderate

☐ Moderately Aggressive   ☐ Aggressive   ☐ Other:_____

7. Fees and expenses (stated as an annual percentage):

Mortality and expense risk charge: _____

Administrative fees: _____

8. List any rider(s) you are recommending, the fee(s) and what the rider(s) guarantees:

Rider: _____ Fee: _____

Guarantee: _____ Fee: _____

Rider: _____ Fee: _____

Guarantee: _____ Fee: _____

Rider: _____ Fee: _____

Guarantee: _____ Fee: _____

10. Does the rider(s) limit my choice of sub-accounts or have other restrictions?

☐ Yes ☐ No

If "yes", explain: _____

_____

11. Can the rider(s) be dropped during the contract period?

☐ Yes ☐ No

12. Total estimated costs of the annuity:

Mortality and expense charges + administrative fees + weighted average expense of the recommended sub-account(s) + rider(s).   State as a percentage.

_____ %

13. Length of contract (after which surrender charges do not apply):

Years: _____

14. Surrender charge by year (stated as a percentage and as a dollar amount of the original premium amount):

Yr 1: % ____ $_____   2: % ____ $_____   3: % ____ $_____

Yr 4: % ____ $_____   5: % ____ $_____   6: % ____ $_____

Yr 7: % ____ $_____   8: % ____ $_____   9: % ____ $_____

Yr 10: % ____ $_____   11: % ____ $_____   12: % ____ $_____

Yr 13: % ____ $_____   14: % ____ $_____   15: % ____ $_____

15. Are penalty-free withdrawals available during surrender period?

☐ Yes ☐ No

Terms/conditions: _____

_____

16. Is there a Long-term Care waiver or rider associated with the annuity?

☐ Yes ☐ No

Terms/conditions: _____

_____

17. Is there a wavier associated with terminal illness?

☐ Yes ☐ No

Terms/conditions: _____

_____

18. "Free look" period:

Period: _____

Buying a Mutual Fund

Know What You're Buying and Why

Checklist

Mutual Fund: Know What You're Buying and Why   p. 53

How Long Does it Take to Do?

About 25 minutes. Your financial advisor provides all the information.

When to Use

☐ Use whenever a mutual fund (or funds) is being recommended to you. It provides a way for your financial advisor to summarize important information about the mutual fund, and explain why the fund is right for you.

KNOW WHAT YOU'RE BUYING, AND WHY

Notes

☐ If you <u>are not</u> already working with the financial advisor who is recommending the mutual fund, use the following two guides <u>first</u>:

☐ Guide: *Financial Advisors: An Overview*   p. 54

☐ Guide: *Financial Advisors: Finding Mr. or Ms. "Right"*   p. 61
Checklist: *Finding Mr. or Ms. "Right"*, Part 1 & Part 2   p. 64 and p. 73

KNOW WHO YOU'RE WORKING WITH. YOU CAN'T AFFORD TO GET INTO THE WRONG RELATIONSHIP

☐ Photocopy the checklist before using.

Buying a Mutual Fund

Dear advisor: just a few questions...

Instructions

Using the checklist:

☐ READ THROUGH THE CHECKLIST INSTRUCTIONS BEFORE USING

☐ Use during a meeting or phone call with your financial advisor. Your advisor provides all the information to complete the checklist. You fill in the answers.

☐ For questions 3, 6, 7 and 10 (if applicable), have your advisor answer using key phrases.

☐ Repeat what you've written back to your advisor.

☐ Financial advisors have a regulatory obligation to answer your questions to your level of satisfaction. You can't afford a fuzzy understanding of what's going on with your money!

What do I say to my advisor?

Using your own words, here's what you want to convey: *"To help me better understand why the mutual fund you're recommending is right for me, I'd appreciate it if you'd answer the questions I have on my checklist. Your willingness to do this goes a long way in showing me that I come first in our relationship, and that the trust and confidence I'm placing in you is well-founded."*

Notes:

☐ While your financial advisor may provide you with a mutual fund report or fact sheet that contains much of the information your checklist requests,

- only your checklists promote and <u>protect your interests</u> with a set of questions from <u>your side</u> of the relationship,

- only your checklists equip you with questions that <u>apply specifically</u> to the decisions and actions of your financial advisor,

- only your checklists help you evaluate the <u>intent</u> of your financial advisor, and the <u>quality and professionalism</u> of your advisor, by how your questions are answered,

- only your checklists allow you to <u>record and file</u> your financial advisor's direct responses to your questions.

☐ The checklist questions are based on industry "best practices" for disclosure. There are no "zinger" or "gotcha" questions.

☐ Beware of evasive answers or claims that it's "against company policy" to answer.

After completion:

☐ Review for accuracy and completeness with your financial advisor.

☐ File the completed checklist in your *My Best Interests* folder.

Your Financial Advisor

Your advisor will explain the importance of each question, and provide you with complete and accurate answers. If additional questions arise, don't be afraid to ask. Your advisor welcomes every opportunity to show you that you come first in the relationship. Completing the checklist is one way to show it.

Let's go over the questions on the checklist:

1. **What is the mutual fund's classification or category?**

    ? What does a good answer look like?

    It's a simple description. A good answer is one that gives you a clear understanding of the types of investments inside the fund. For example, a stock/equity mutual fund may be described as "Domestic Large Growth" or "Small Cap Value", depending on the types of stocks inside the fund.

    Note: Classification/category descriptions vary among mutual fund rating/ranking services.

    Choosing a mutual fund by its classification or category is a lot like choosing a roller coaster ride. There are slow and easy roller coasters, and there are big and fast ones. Also, the same type of roller coaster can have different names at different parks. It's the same with mutual funds. You may own funds with different names from different fund families, but they could all be in the same kind of fund offering you the same kind of ride. You may not be as diversified as you think. Blending the rides together may balance out the extremes and offer a manageable ride at an acceptable speed to achieve your goals.

2. **Is the fund suitable for me?**

     This is the most important question on the checklist.

    Most of us expect our financial advisor to do what's right for us. "Doing what's right" is intuitive. We don't need legal definitions to know what it means and the intent behind it. But there is one regulatory term you need to know about: "suitability".

    " *Suitability?"*

    > **"** *Suitability" is regulatory-speak for "doing what's right".*
    > *Your advisor has a <u>regulatory obligation</u> to only recommend*
    > *mutual funds that are suitable or "right" for your needs,*
    > *financial situation, investment objective, risk tolerance, etc."*

    ? Okay, so what does a good answer look like?
    A direct "yes" is the only acceptable answer.

    Going beyond the rules, if you don't understand the mutual fund, or it doesn't make sense to you, it probably isn't right for you.

3. What criteria did you use to select the fund?

Your financial advisor may use several criteria for selecting mutual funds.

? What does a good answer look like?

<u>It doesn't need to be lengthy or complicated</u>. All you need are a few key phrases that describe how your advisor selected the fund. Note: If past performance is the only criteria your advisor used, it's *not* a good answer.

Your Financial Advisor

Your advisor knows that past performance isn't a reliable indicator of future performance, and shouldn't be used as the sole criterion for a recommendation. "Hot" funds often follow with a period of under-performance.

4. What is the inception date of the fund?

? What does a good answer look like?

It's more than just entering the date. If it's a new fund, you want to know why your advisor would place you in a fund with little or no track record. Note: Many advisors use inception date as a filter in selecting mutual funds. Why? Because funds that have been in business for several years provide more data for an advisor to evaluate than do funds with short track records.

5. What is the manager/management team's tenure?

? What does a good answer look like?

As with #4, it's more than just entering the date. If the fund manager(s) is new, you want to know why your advisor would place you in a fund with a manager(s) with little or no track record. Many advisors use management tenure as one of their criteria for selecting funds. Fund managers with multiple-decade track records and experience through several "bull" and "bear" market cycles are generally preferred over un-proven managers or managers with short track records.

6. How does the fund fit in with other investments I own? (If applicable)

? What does a good answer look like?

Buying a new fund just for the sake of buying a new fund isn't good business. It could also bring additional expenses you could have avoided. A good answer will explain how the new fund fits in with other investments you already own. For example, does it bring further diversification? Does it increase the potential for growth? Does it provide additional income? Does it reduce risk? A few key phrases are all you need.

7. What share class are you recommending and why?

Most mutual funds offer several share classes. The two most popular share classes used by full-service financial advisors are Class A shares and Class C shares. Important note: <u>Class A and Class C shares have very different cost/fee structures</u>. There are instances where Class A shares may be more appropriate than Class C shares, and instances where Class C shares may be justifiable.

" Share classes… really?"

" Your advisor has a <u>regulatory obligation</u> to make sure you understand what share class is being used and how it works. You can't afford a fuzzy understanding of what's going on with your money!"

? What does a good answer look like?

Your advisor needs to explain the share class being used, and why it's suitable for you. This explanation should take into account:

1. The dollar amount of your investment
2. How long you anticipate holding the fund
3. Your advisor's investment strategy (especially for Class C shares)

<u>Your advisor's explanation doesn't need to be complicated to be a good answer</u>. A few key phrases are all it takes.

8. What does it cost to buy the fund?

? What does a good answer look like?

A good answer will disclose the sales charge that applies to your initial investment stated as a percentage and as a dollar amount. For example, a front-end sales charge of 3% on a $1 investment would reduce the amount invested into the fund by 3¢ for a net investment of $97. If, for example, your investment was $1,000, the front-end charge would total $30 (or 3¢ per dollar). This would make your actual investment into the fund $970. Refer to Quick Course: *Calculating Total Costs,* p. 133, for more information.

9. What are the breakpoints?

Most funds offering Class A shares offer discounts that reduce the front-end sales charge. These discounts are based on the dollar amount of the investment, and are called "breakpoints". The first breakpoint is typically at $25,000 or $50,000 depending on the fund.

? What does a good answer look like?

If your advisor is recommending Class A shares, he or she will disclose what the breakpoint schedule is for the fund. (It's also in the fund prospectus). If your advisor is recommending Class C shares of a mutual fund, breakpoints do not apply. Note: It's important that you and your advisor plan fund purchases to take advantage of breakpoints within a fund family.

10. Is there a cost to sell the fund?

Some funds charge shareholders if they liquidate shares within a certain number of years. This is referred to as a "back-end" or "deferred" charge.

? What does a good answer look like?

A good answer will disclose any deferred sales charge and the terms. For example: "1% deferred sales charge if sold within a 12-month period". In this example, if you sold $1,000 of the fund within 12 months of the date you bought the fund, your net proceeds from the sale would be $990 ($1,000 - $10 or 1%).

11. What is the fund's expense ratio? How does it compare to funds in the same group or category?

The expense ratio is the fund's cost of doing business that's passed on to you, the shareholder. You want to know three things:

1. The fund's expense ratio.

2. How it compares to the average expense ratio for funds in the same group or category? Is it the most expensive? Is it a low-expense fund? <u>Excessive fees are money out of your pocket.</u>

3. What the range of expense ratios is within that fund group or category. Using these ratios as examples, your checklist will look like this:

Fund's Expense Ratio: __**0.79%**__ Category Ave: __**0.95%**__ Range: __**0.11%**__ to __**2.13%**__

Note: Your full-service advisor has easy access to expense ratio information.

? What does a good answer look like?

A good answer provides all four figures. <u>They allow you to gauge how your fund's expenses compare with other funds in the same category</u>. Note: Your advisor may use fund expenses as a criteria for selecting mutual funds. In general, funds with lower expenses are preferred over funds with higher expenses. If the fund being recommended to you has a higher than average expense ratio, your advisor may have a valid justification for recommending it. Your advisor welcomes the opportunity to explain why.   A few key phrases are all you need.

Note: Mutual funds are sold by prospectus. <u>The *Mutual Fund* checklist does not replace the mutual fund prospectus</u>. Check the box on the checklist when you receive the prospectus.

Your Financial Advisor
Your advisor knows that controlling your costs is always good business.
It's another way for them to show you that you come first in the relationship.

Special Note: Your relationship with your financial advisor should be one of your most important and valuable professional relationships. Your checklist allows you to gauge the quality of this relationship by how your advisor answers your questions. Your checklist also allows you to confirm that your advisor puts you first, and that the relationship is based upon openness, fair play and accountability. <u>You can't afford a relationship that doesn't work this way</u>.

Mutual Fund: Know What You're Buying and Why

Dear advisor: just a few questions...

Date: _____

Name of mutual fund/ETF:_____

1. What is fund's classification or category? _____

2. Is the fund suitable for me?   ☐ Confirmed "yes" by my advisor

3. What criteria did you use to select the fund? _____

   _____

   _____

4. What is the inception date of the fund? _____

5. What is the manager/management team's tenure? _____ years

6. How does the fund fit in with other investments I own?   ☐ Not applicable

   _____

   _____

7. What share class are recommending and why?   ☐ Class A   ☐ Class C   ☐ Other

   Explanation:_____

   _____

8. What does it cost to buy the fund?   Sales Charge: _____% $_____
   Based upon dollar amount of the initial investment

9. What is the breakpoint schedule?   ☐ Not applicable

   _____

9. Is there a cost to sell the fund?   ☐ Yes   ☐ No

   If "yes", what are the terms? _____

10. What is the fund's expense ratio? How does it compare to funds in the same category?

   Fund's Expense Ratio: _____   Category Ave: _____   Range: _____ to _____

Financial Advisors

An Overview

When to Use

☐ Use this guide to familiarize yourself with the various types of financial advisors, the services and products they offer, and the standard of care each type is held to in the handling of client/customer accounts.

☐ To help you determine which type of financial advisor may be right for your financial circumstances, needs and preferences.

☐ To know more about your current financial advisor.

KNOW WHICH TYPE OF FINANCIAL ADVISOR IS RIGHT FOR YOU

Applies To

☐ Full-service advisors affiliated with a retirement plan provider

☐ Full-service advisors at banks and credit unions

☐ Full-service advisors at brokerage firms

☐ Advisors at Registered Investment Adviser (RIA) firms

☐ Insurance agents

Note

☐ "Financial advisor" is a generic term for insurance agent, registered representative (broker), registered investment adviser (RIA), investment adviser rep (IAR) and non-legal terms such as investment executive, financial consultant, wealth manager and financial planner.

Financial Advisors
An Overview

This guide will familiarize you with three types of financial advisors:

- ☐ Insurance Agent
- ☐ Registered Representative (broker)
- ☐ Registered Investment Advisor (RIA)

Insurance Agents

Insurance agents are in the business of recommending and selling insurance and insurance-related investment products to their customers. In general, there are two broad categories of insurance agents: independent agents who represent several insurance companies and exclusive agents who represent only one insurance company. In both categories, the agent acts as a representative or "agent" of the insurance company when dealing with customers.

Standard of Care
An insurance agent /producer has a duty to use reasonable care, diligence, and judgment in procuring insurance for you. Important Note: Even if you rely on an agent's expertise, you still have a duty to read the policy documents for deficiencies.

Regulation and Oversight
Insurance agents are regulated by the state(s) in which they do business. Agents who sell mutual funds or variable annuities, are also regulated by the Financial Industry Regulatory Authority (FINRA). The National Association of Insurance Commissioners or NAIC is a standard-setting and regulatory support organization created and governed by state insurance regulators. Through the NAIC, state insurance regulators establish standards and best practices, conduct peer review, and coordinate their regulatory oversight.

Legal Titles
Insurance agent, producer, producing agent

Non-legal Titles
Advisor, financial planner, financial advisor

Example Products Offered

- ☐ Fixed, indexed, and variable annuities
- ☐ Cash value, term, universal and variable life insurance
- ☐ Long term care insurance
- ☐ Disability insurance
- ☐ Mutual funds (if properly licensed)

Compensation
Generally commission-based. The above-referenced products are examples of products that generally pay a sales commission to the agent/advisor.

Note: Certain insurance products allow the agent to opt for an ongoing fee instead of an up-front commission.

Registered Representatives / Brokers

Brokers are legally referred to as registered representatives, meaning they are properly licensed and registered to buy and sell securities for their customers through the company they represent. The company is known as the broker/dealer. Brokers typically earn a commission when buying and selling securities inside their customers' accounts.

 Registered representatives must have all buys and sells approved by the account owner before the transaction can take place. This type of account is known as a "non-discretionary" account. This is why registered reps or "brokers" are always on the phone with their customers making buy and sell recommendations and confirming approval for each transaction.

Standard of Care: "Suitability"

Most of us expect our registered representative/broker to do what's right for us. "Doing what's right" is intuitive. We don't need legal definitions to know what it means and the intentions behind it. But there is one regulatory term you need to know about: "suitability". In regulatory-speak, "doing what's right" is called "suitability". This means your broker has a regulatory obligation to have a reasonable basis for believing that the recommendation is suitable or "right" for your needs, financial situation, investment objective, risk tolerance, etc.

 The suitability standard has its shortcomings:

☐ A registered rep/broker can sell you a second-rate and higher-cost investment product and still be "within the rules" of the suitability standard.

☐ A registered rep/broker can deliberately generate commissions from your account and still be "within the rules" in the suitability standard.

☐ Conflicts of interests between your registered rep/broker and you may not violate the suitability standard.

Special Note: The "suitability" standard of care does not guarantee protection from abusive sales practices and self-serving registered representatives. So the best way to look out for your best interests is to ask questions about all investments and strategies being recommended to you, and make sure that your questions are answered to your level of satisfaction. Also, be aware of what's going on in your account. Review your statements and trade confirmations for accuracy and report any discrepancies or unusual activity to your registered rep/broker.

Regulation and Oversight

Registered representatives/brokers are regulated by the state securities regulators in each state in which they do business. They are also regulated by the Financial Industry Regulatory Authority or FINRA and the Securities and Exchange Commission or SEC.

Legal Title

Registered Representative

Non-legal Titles

Stockbroker, investment executive, financial consultant and wealth manager.

Example Products/Investments Offered

- ☐ Individual stocks and bonds
- ☐ Mutual Funds
- ☐ Exchange-traded funds (ETF)
- ☐ Initial Public Offerings or IPOs
- ☐ Annuities and other insurance-related products - if licensed

Compensation

Generally commission-based. The above-referenced products are examples of products that typically pay a sales commission to the registered representative.

Is a Registered Rep/Broker Right for You?

The answer could be "yes" if you agree with most of the following:

- ☐ You're only interested in "buy" and "sell" recommendations from your broker.
- ☐ You have above-average investment knowledge and experience, and you like being involved with your broker in making investment decisions.
- ☐ You what to authorize each buy or sell in your account prior to execution.
- ☐ You typically "buy and hold" your investments.
- ☐ You trade infrequently.
- ☐ Paying a fair commission is an acceptable way to compensate your broker.

Registered Investment Advisers

Registered investment advisers (RIAs) provide ongoing advice to their clients. In general, RIAs use the same investments offered by the registered representative. But instead of buying and selling investments for a commission, investments are managed for an advisory fee.

A RIA can be a stand-alone independent firm or part of a large financial institution. Advisers who provide advice to their clients through their financial institution's RIA, are referred to as investment adviser reps (IARs). Most large full-service brokerage firms have a registered broker/dealer unit and a registered investment adviser.

If properly licensed, a financial advisor can be a registered representative, an investment adviser representative and even an insurance agent all at the same time. This is referred to as being "dually licensed", and is common among financial advisors working at large brokerage firms.

Standard of Care: "Fiduciary"

RIAs and IARs have a duty of loyalty and are obligated to act in your best interests. In regulatory-speak, this is referred to as acting as a "fiduciary". Acting as a fiduciary, every consideration, decision and transaction must be made exclusively for your benefit without regard to the financial interests or other interests of your RIA/IAR. Any conflicts of interest must be fully-disclosed up front. It is the highest standard of care in the financial services industry.

Unlike "non-discretionary" transactions that require registered representatives to have all transactions approved by the customer prior to execution, RIAs may transact business on a "discretionary" basis. This means they have authority and approval to buy and sell securities and to make other investment-related decisions on behalf of their clients without receiving prior approval. Granting discretion to the adviser is part of the advisory agreement and must be plainly spelled-out.

 The fiduciary standard doesn't guarantee protection from unethical practices.

Special Note: The fiduciary standard doesn't guarantee protection from unethical practices. You can't assume that an adviser held to the fiduciary standard is necessarily more ethical than an insurance agent or registered representative held to the suitability standard. It all comes down to the integrity and intent of the individual adviser. So ask questions and be aware of what's going on with your account.

Regulation and Oversight
State securities regulators for RIAs with assets under $100 million.
The Securities and Exchange Commission (SEC) for RIAs with assets over $100 million.

Legal Title
Registered investment adviser (RIA) or investment adviser representative (IAR)

Example Products/Investments Offered

- ☐ Mutual fund "wrap" (fee-based) accounts
- ☐ Separately managed accounts or SMAs through outside investment management firms
- ☐ Individual stocks
- ☐ Individual bonds
- ☐ Exchange-traded funds (ETF)

Compensation

- ☐ Asset-based fee (a.k.a. advisory fee) typically stated as an annual percentage based upon the value of the account.
- ☐ Flat dollar amount based upon the size of the account or the complexity of the account.
- ☐ Hourly rate billed monthly or quarterly
- ☐ Project retainer fee / monthly subscription

Is an RIA or IAR right for you?
The answer could be "yes" if you agree with most of the following:

- ☐ You require or want ongoing advice.

- ☐ You require or are more comfortable with the fiduciary standard of care rather than the lower suitability standard of care.

- ☐ You require or want comprehensive reporting and performance measurement.

- ☐ You require or want the adviser to make investment transactions on your behalf without you having to authorize each transaction.

- ☐ You are required to pay, or prefer to pay a fee for services.

Note: If you are a trustee or guardian who is responsible for the oversight and monitoring of investments for an individual, organization or other entity, you may be required to work with a RIA or IAR who is obligated to the fiduciary standard of care.

General Comparison

Item:	Registered Representative:	RIA or IAR:
Other titles:	"Stockbroker", "Wealth Manager", etc.	"Adviser"
Transactions:	Non-discretionary trading	Discretionary trading
Compensation:	Commission-based	Fee-based
Standard of Care:	Suitability	Fiduciary

Financial Planners (non-legal term)

"Financial planner" is not a legal term. It's a description. In general, financial planners are in the business of developing comprehensive financial plans for their clients. So an insurance agent, a registered rep, and a registered investment adviser can all be "financial planners" within the scope that their licensing permits.

Are Other Financial-Related Services Right for You?

While investment management is the primary service provided by most registered reps/brokers, RIAs and IARs, many are credentialed experts who offer other important financial-related services. These can include:

- ☐ College planning
- ☐ Financial planning
- ☐ Insurance planning
- ☐ Tax-efficient investment strategies
- ☐ IRA/retirement plan withdrawal strategies
- ☐ Legacy and generational planning
- ☐ Special needs planning
- ☐ Post-divorce planning

If you'd like one-stop access to these types of services through your financial advisor, make sure your advisor has the expertise to provide them to you. Just because your advisor has the ability to generate a plan or report through their brokerage/advisory firm doesn't mean your advisor is an expert. Having an advisor with specialized training may be important to you.

Professional Designations

Some advisors choose to take specialized coursework in order to earn a professional designation. But not all professional designations are created equal. Some require rigorous coursework over a several-month or several-year period, while others can be acquired more easily.

To evaluate a professional designation, follow the checklist below. It only takes a few minutes to do, and the information will help you determine whether the designation has any value or application to your financial situation.

- ☐ Visit the website of the organization issuing the designation

- ☐ Know the prerequisites and coursework for obtaining the designation

- ☐ Know the continuing education requirements

- ☐ Know if an investor complaint or public disciplinary process exists

- ☐ Know if the designation has third-party accreditation

Some states require designations to be accredited in order to be used in their state. For more information on professional designations, you can visit the FINRA website at www.finra.org Tools & Calculators, Understanding Professional Designations.

Financial Advisors

Finding Mr. or Ms. "Right"

Checklist

"Finding Mr. or Ms. "Right" Part 1: Completed by you p. 64
"Finding Mr. or Ms. "Right" Part 2: Completed by the advisor p. 73

How Long Does it Take to Do?

About 15 minutes for you to complete Part 1 of the checklist.
About one hour to go over Part 2 with the financial advisor. It's time well spent.

When to Use

☐ When you want to evaluate a financial advisor you're considering doing business with, or

☐ To re-evaluate or know more about your current advisor.

KNOW WHO YOU'RE WORKING WITH. YOU CAN'T AFFORD TO GET INTO THE WRONG RELATIONSHIP

Applies To

☐ Full-service advisors affiliated with a retirement plan provider

☐ Full-service advisors at banks and credit unions

☐ Full-service advisors at brokerage firms

☐ Advisors at Registered Investment Adviser (RIA) firms

☐ Insurance agents

Important Note

☐ If you <u>are not</u> already working with the advisor, read the following guide <u>first</u>:

☐ Guide: *Financial Advisors: An Overview* p. 54

☐ Photocopy the two checklists before using.

Financial Advisors:
Finding Mr. or Ms. "Right"

What to Know

Your relationship with a financial advisor can be one of your most important and valuable professional relationships. The nature of the relationship, the intent of your advisor, and the measurable competency of your advisor can have a tremendous impact on your financial well-being over what may be a multiple-decade relationship. Regardless of whether the relationship only involves your investments or is broader in scope and more complex, *you must come first* in the relationship.

How does a financial advisor show that you come first?   It's simple: three attributes need to show up in the relationship:

☐ Openness
☐ Fair Play
☐ Accountability

These attributes are intuitive, and apply to any important personal or professional relationship. When this combination of inter-relationship decency and business ethics are present, a fourth attribute of a quality relationship shows up:

☐ Trust

You can't afford a relationship that doesn't work this way.

Finding Mr. or Ms. "Right"

Where do you start looking for the right financial advisor for you? Sources for finding financial advisors to interview include:

☐ Brokerage/advisory firm websites. These websites allow you to locate a branch office in your area. Typically, the branch office website posts the bios and credentials of the brokers/advisers in that office.

☐ Organizations that issue professional designations. To learn about professional designations, visit the FINRA website at www.finra.org and click on Tools & Calculators, then Understanding Professional Designations. If you think a particular professional designation may be of value to your financial situation, visit the website of the issuing organization. Typically these websites allow you to search for designation holders in your area.

The *Finding Mr. or Ms. "Right"* checklists will help you to find the investment profession who is best suited to enter into this vitally-important relationship with you. Let's get started.

Checklist Instructions
Part 1: Questions to Ask Yourself

The *Finding Mr. or Ms. "Right"* checklist has two parts: Part 1 is for you to complete before you interview a new advisor or re-evaluate your current advisor, and Part 2 is for the advisor to complete.

Not Yet Working with a Financial Advisor

☐ If you are not working with a financial advisor, Part 1 will help you assess your needs and preferences, and help you decide which type of advisor may be right for you.

☐ It's important for you complete Part 1 prior to having a financial advisor complete Part 2. It will allow you to evaluate the advisor's responses in light of your responses in Part 1.

Established Relationship with a Financial Advisor

☐ If you have an established relationship with a financial advisor, Part 1 will help you assess whether your needs and preferences have changed since you started working with your advisor.

☐ After your advisor completes Part 2, you can evaluate his or her responses in light of your responses in Part 1 to determine whether your current advisor is still Mr. or Ms. "Right".

After completion:

File the completed checklist in your *My Best Interests* folder.

Part 1
Questions to Ask Yourself

Recommendations or Ongoing Advice?

Yes No
☐ ☐ Are you only interested in occasional investment recommendations from your advisor?

Yes No
☐ ☐ Do you have above-average investment knowledge and experience, and like being involved with your advisor in making investment decisions?

Yes No
☐ ☐ Do you what to authorize each buy or sell in your account prior to execution?

Yes No
☐ ☐ Do you typically "buy and hold" your investments?

Yes No
☐ ☐ Do you trade infrequently?

Yes No
☐ ☐ Is paying a commission an acceptable way to compensate your advisor?

Note: If you answered "yes" to most of the above questions, a registered representative or "broker" may be the right choice for your financial circumstances, needs and preferences.

Yes No
☐ ☐ Do you want ongoing investment advice from your financial advisor?

Yes No
☐ ☐ Do you want your advisor to make investment transactions on your behalf without you having to authorize each transaction?

Yes No
☐ ☐ Do you want your advisor held to a fiduciary standard of care in the handling of Your account rather than the lower suitability standard of care?

Yes No
☐ ☐ Is paying a fee for services an acceptable way to compensate your advisor?

Note: If you answered "yes" to most of these four questions, a registered investment adviser (RIA) or investment adviser rep (IAR) may be the right choice for your needs and preferences.

Types of Investments

Yes No

☐ ☐ Do you like the features, benefits and guarantees offered through insurance-related investment products such as life insurance and annuities?

Yes No

☐ ☐ Are you comfortable investing in broadly-diversified investment options like mutual funds and exchange-traded funds (ETF)?

Yes No

☐ ☐ Are you comfortable investing in individual stocks and bonds?

Yes No

☐ ☐ Are you interested in socially responsible investing?

Note: Knowing what types of investments you're comfortable with is important. For example, if you like the benefits and guarantees of annuities, then make sure you're working with an agent/advisor who is licensed to sell insurance-related products. If you like individual stocks and bonds, then working with an insurance agent may not be the right choice for you. If you prefer broadly-diversified investments like mutual funds and ETFs, then working with a broker who only deals with individual stocks and bonds may not be the right choice for you. And if you would like a socially-responsible approach to investing, then make sure the financial advisor espouses your values, and that his or her investment management practices are aligned with generally-accepted principles of socially-responsible investing.

Other Services

While investment management is the primary service provided by most registered reps/brokers, RIAs and IARs, many are credentialed experts who offer other important financial-related services. Use this list to check-off other services that are important to you now, or may be important to you in the future.

Yes No

☐ ☐ College planning services?

Yes No

☐ ☐ Financial planning?

Yes No

☐ ☐ Insurance planning?

Yes No

☐ ☐ Tax-efficient investment strategies?

Yes No

☐ ☐ IRA/retirement plan withdrawal strategies?

Yes No

☐   ☐   Legacy and generational planning?

Yes No

☐   ☐   Special needs planning?

Yes No

☐   ☐   Post-divorce planning?

Note: If you answered "yes" to some of these, make sure your current financial advisor, or the advisor you're considering working with is capable of providing those services as an <u>expert.</u> Having an advisor with specialized training may be important to you.

Customer Service and Communication

Another component to consider when evaluating financial advisors is customer service and communication. Ask yourself these questions:

Would you like online access to your accounts?

☐ Yes   ☐ No

In what form would you like to receive your monthly statements?

☐ Traditional paper statements   ☐ Paperless

Would you like to access information about your account online or through an app?

☐ Yes   ☐ No

Would you like to receive a statement for each account or a consolidated statement?

☐ Individual statement   ☐ Consolidated statement   ☐ Not applicable

How often or at what interval would you like to be contacted either verbally or in writing/e-mail?

☐ Monthly

☐ Quarterly (minimum)

☐ As needed during the month or quarter

Method of communication: (Check all that apply)

☐ Home phone   ☐ Office phone
☐ Cell phone   ☐ E-mail

If your advisor is unavailable when you call, what is an acceptable timeframe for them to return your call?

☐ Same day, if possible   ☐ 24 hrs.   ☐ 48 hrs.

How often or at what interval would you like an in-person meeting with your advisor?

- ☐ Monthly
- ☐ Quarterly
- ☐ Annually
- ☐ As needed during the month or quarter

Who else would you like to receive statements or receive formal communications from your advisor? (Check all that apply)

- ☐ Attorney
- ☐ CPA
- ☐ Trustee
- ☐ Family members

Note: when you are interviewing a financial advisor, take note of the receptionist and assistants who may be handling your service requests. How they interact with you and the quality of their service is an important consideration.

Conflicts of Interests

This is most important question:

Do you want to work with a financial advisor who will put you first in the relationship, and not advance their interests or those of their company at your expense?

☐ Yes   ☐ No

You've completed **Part 1**. Use this this as a reference when you interview advisor candidates, or if you are re-evaluating your current financial advisor.

Next is **Part 2**.

Checklist Instructions
Part 2: Questions to Ask the Financial Advisor

Not Yet Working with a Financial Advisor

If you are not working with a financial advisor, Part 2 provides a great way for you to:

☐ Separate weaker, less competent advisors from stronger, more competent ones.

☐ Identify advisors whose business model and services are more aligned with your needs and preferences.

☐ Alert you to advisors who may be incompatible with your personality, preferences and values.

Note: The best way to complete Part 2 is during your initial meeting with the advisor. An alternative is to email/mail it to him or her to complete and return to you prior to setting a meeting. If you decide to move forward and meet with the advisor, bring along your completed Part 1. It will serve as a handy reference for you and the advisor.

Established Relationship with a Financial Advisor

☐ If you have an established relationship with an advisor, Part 2 is best completed during a meeting with him or her.

☐ Be sure to bring along your completed Part 1. It will serve as a reference for you and your financial advisor, and may provide additional clarity and understanding that strengthens the relationship.

☐ Comparing Part 1 with Part 2 may also alert you to shortfalls or gaps between what your needs and preferences are, and what your financial advisor can expertly provide.

Note: Changes in your financial circumstances may bring complexities that require expertise beyond your advisor abilities. The fact that your advisor is able to create a plan or generate a report through their brokerage/advisory firm doesn't mean he or she is an expert. It is not uncommon to outgrow a financial advisor.

After completion:
File the completed checklists in your *My Best Interests* folder.

Finding Mr. or Ms. "Right"
The Importance of the Checklist Questions in Part 2

Let's go over the questions on the checklist:

1. What are your clients like?

? What does a good answer look like?

Are there general similarities between your financial needs and preferences and those of the advisor's clients?

Why is this important? If, for example, you're seeking comprehensive financial planning and prefer investing in lower-risk mutual funds, and the financial advisor's clients are aggressive stock traders, you're definitely not going to fit in!

2. As their advisor, how do you view your role with them?

Some advisors will have a narrow view of their role with clients. It may be limited to investment management and providing research, insight and recommendations on investment and market-related matters. Other advisors may take a deeper and more spacious view of their role. In this instance, the advisor may provide services and advice that go beyond investment management to include financial, insurance and legacy planning, or specialized services and advice on family-related matters like special needs and post-divorce planning.

? What does a good answer look like?

One that expresses what you're looking for in a business relationship with a financial advisor.

3. What is your educational and professional background?

Note: While many firms require their advisors to have a bachelor's degree, many advisors do not. A financial advisor can be highly-qualified and regarded as an expert without having a college degree.

4. Do you have professional designations or other credentials?

Some advisors choose to take specialized coursework in order to earn a professional designation. Why may this be important to you? Depending on your financial situation and needs, advisors with certain professional designations may be of value to you. For example, an advisor with a professional designation in financial planning may be regarded as more qualified to provide this service to you than an advisor without the designation.

5. What standard of care will apply to my account?

 In the handling of your account, your financial advisor has a duty of care and loyalty. There are two standards of care that apply to financial advisors: the "suitability" standard and the "fiduciary" standard.

Under the "suitability" standard of care, your advisor has a regulatory obligation to have a reasonable basis for believing that the recommendation, strategy or transaction is suitable or appropriate for your needs, financial situation, investment objective, risk tolerance, investment experience, etc.

Under the "fiduciary" standard of care, every consideration, decision and transaction must be made exclusively for your benefit without regard to the financial interests or other interests of your advisor. Any conflicts of interest must be fully-disclosed up front. The fiduciary standard is the highest standard of care in the financial services industry.

For more information refer to the guide titled *Financial Advisors: an Overview*. Under "Registered Representatives" is a description of the suitability standard of care. And on the next page under "Registered Investment Advisers" is a description of the fiduciary standard of care.

Note: Regardless of the standard of care the financial advisor is held to, <u>it all comes down to the reliability, honesty and intent of the individual advisor.</u> So the best way to look out for your own interests is to <u>ask the right questions</u> and be aware of what's going on with your account.

6. Will you put me first in our relationship, and not advance your interests or those of your company at my expense?

 Question 5 is about the <u>regulatory</u> standards that apply to the handling your account. This question is about the terms of your <u>relationship</u> with your advisor.

Note: With every recommendation and every action, your financial advisor makes a conscious decision to either put you first, or their own interests first. <u>News Flash: regulations and "standard of care" rules do not guide this decision.</u> It's guided by personal integrity, or by the absence of this trait.

? What does a good answer look like?

A direct "yes" is the only acceptable answer. You can't afford to enter into a relationship with a financial advisor who won't put you first.

7. What types of investments might you use in my account?

Waiting until after you open an account to find this out isn't good business. In most instances, the advisor has a good idea of what types of investments will end up in your account. (See "Types of Investments" on page 2 of Part 1 of the checklist in this guide.)

Note: If your advisor recommends an annuity, he or she must also complete the appropriate *Buying an Annuity* checklist before you make a decision. Also, if your account is commission-based and your advisor recommends mutual funds, he or she must also complete the *Buying a Mutual Fund* checklist for each fund being recommended. Note: This does not apply to fee-based accounts.

8. How will you receive compensation for handling my account?

Depending on whether your account is commission-based, fee-based or fee-only, your advisor can receive compensation in different ways. For example, if your account is commission-based, your advisor may receive compensation from items "A" through "E" (see checklist on page 73). If your advisor is also licensed to sell insurance products, he or she may also receive compensation for item "F". If your account is fee-based, your advisor will typically receive item "G" compensation. If your advisor is also licensed to sell insurance products, he or she may also receive compensation through item "F".

? What does a good answer look like?

You expect your advisor to disclose all potential sources of compensation. Confirm with your advisor that all applicable boxes are checked. If your account is going to be fee-based or fee-only, you expect the applicable percentage (for advisory fees based upon the assets under management), hourly rate, or other terms for payment to be disclosed.

9. Who else may be handling my account?

Your advisor may be part of a team or group. And while he or she may be your primary advisor, you may interact with other members of the team/group.

? What does a good answer look like?

Most advisors will introduce you to all the members of their group and also introduce you to the sales assistant(s) and receptionist. All you need for your checklist are the names of the individuals you will most likely interact with you on a frequent basis.

10. Will you disclose all costs associated with the handling of my account at least annually?

? What does a good answer look like?

A direct "yes". Note: "All costs" should include commissions, any mark-up/mark-downs and any mutual fund/ETF internal expenses.

You will use the *Total Costs* guide(s) and checklist(s) with your advisor at least annually. Also, refer to Quick Course: *Calculating Total Costs,* p. 133, for more information.

11. Will you provide a performance report on my account that is measured against an appropriate benchmark at least annually?

If your account is with a commission-based broker (registered representative), he or she can typically generate an "on demand" performance report on your account right from their computer. They may, however, be prohibited by company policy from calculating a benchmark return to compare your account's return against. If your advisor can't calculate a benchmark return, there's a workaround: you can do the calculations yourself. It only takes a few minutes, and the math is easy. Refer to Quick Courses: *Calculating Returns,* p. 127, and *Benchmarking Returns,* p. 129.

If your account is fee-based, you'll typically receive a report that includes your account's return compared against a benchmark that represents how your account is invested. While this report provides valuable information, only your checklist promotes and protects your interests with a set of specific questions from your side of the relationship.

? What does a good answer look like?

A direct "yes".

12. What information or reports on my account can I get online or in an app?

Most brokerage/advisory firms offer online access to information about your account. Statements and trade confirmations are also available online. If this is important to you, be sure to sign-up.

13. What other services do you provide?

While skillful management of your investments is always important, you may have other financial-related needs that are equally important to you.

? What does a good answer look like?

You want to see boxes checked next to those services you may need or anticipate needing. While most advisors provide these services for no additional charge, some advisors do charge a fee. Make sure the fee is disclosed.

13b. In providing these services, are you regarded as an expert?

Note: The fact that your advisor is able to create a plan or generate a report through their brokerage/advisory firm or a third party doesn't mean your advisor is an expert. Having an advisor with specialized training may be important to you.

? What does a good answer look like?

A direct "yes".

14. When was your advisory firm/brokerage office last audited by FINRA or SEC?

Why is this important? Many smaller registered investment advisory firms haven't been audited in years. While this doesn't imply anything, you may find comfort in knowing that your advisor's brokerage/advisory firm has been recently audited by regulators.

Special Note: Your relationship with your financial advisor should be one of your most important and valuable professional relationships. Your checklist allows you to gauge the quality of this relationship by how your advisor answers your questions. Your checklist also allows you to confirm that your advisor puts you first, and that the relationship is based upon openness, fair play and accountability. <u>You can't afford a relationship that doesn't work this way</u>.

Finding Mr. or Ms. "Right"

Dear advisor: just a few questions...

Part 2
Questions to Ask the Financial Advisor

1. What are your clients like?

   _____

   _____

   _____

   _____

   _____

2. As their advisor, how do you view your role with them?

   _____

   _____

   _____

   _____

   _____

3. What is your educational and professional background?

   _____

   _____

   _____

   _____

4. Do you have professional designations or other credentials?

   ☐ Yes ☐ No

   _____

   _____

5. What "standard of care" will apply to my account?

   ☐ Fiduciary ☐ Suitability

6. Will you put me first in our relationship, and not advance your interests or those of your company at my expense?

☐ Yes ☐ No

7. What types of investments might you use in my account? (Check all that apply)

☐ Individual stocks

☐ Individual bonds

☐ Exchange-traded funds (ETF)

☐ Mutual funds

☐ Annuities and other insurance-related products

☐ Fee-based "managed" account

☐ Other: _____

8. How might you be compensated for managing my account? (Check all that may apply)

☐ A: Commissions from buying and selling of individual stocks, ETFs, etc.

☐ B: Mark-ups and mark-downs from buying and selling of individual bonds

☐ C: Commissions/up-front sales charges on the purchase of mutual funds

☐ D: Sales concessions from new securities offerings

☐ E: "Trailer"/service fees on mutual funds (typically between 0.25% and 1.00%)

☐ F: Commissions on the purchase of annuities and other insurance-related products

☐ G: Advisory fee as a percentage of assets under management: _____%

☐ H: Hourly rate for advisory services: Rate: $_____ an hour

☐ I: Retainer for advisory services: Terms: _____

☐ Other: _____

9. Who else may be handling my account?

Names: _____

10. Will you disclose all costs associated with the handling of my account at least annually?

☐ Yes ☐ No

11. Will you provide a performance report on my account that is measured against an appropriate benchmark at least annually?

☐ Yes ☐ No

12. What information or reports on my account can I get online or in an app?

_____

_____

13. What other services do you provide? (Check all that apply)

- [ ] College planning
- [ ] Financial planning
- [ ] Insurance planning
- [ ] Tax-efficient investment strategies
- [ ] IRA/retirement plan withdrawal strategies
- [ ] Legacy and generational planning
- [ ] Special needs planning
- [ ] Post-divorce planning
- [ ] Other: _____

1. Are there additional costs for these services?

   [ ] Yes [ ] No   If "Yes" $: _____

2. In providing these services, are you regarded as an expert?

   [ ] Yes [ ] No

14. When was your advisory firm/brokerage office last audited by FINRA or SEC?

Month: _____ Year: _____

Note: Most financial advisors have no record of disciplinary action against them. You can confirm this by contacting your state securities regulator at http://www.nasaa.org/about-us/contact-us/contact -your-regulator/ or the Financial Industry Regulatory Authority or FINRA at http://www.finra.org/brokercheck, or the SEC at http://www.sec.gov/investor/brokers.htm.

In the course of doing business, a customer may file a complaint against their financial advisor. Complaints are allegation-driven and may not result in any disciplinary action. If your advisor has a complaint noted on their report, discuss the matter with them before drawing any conclusions.

Your Financial Advisor

Is the Relationship Right?

Checklist

Assessing the Relationship p. 80

How Long Does it Take to Do?

About 15 minutes

When to Use

☐ Use this guide to help you confirm that your financial advisor puts you first in the relationship, and that he or she provides the services most appropriate for your financial situation, needs and preferences.

☐ To re-confirm that your advisor puts <u>you first</u> in the relationship.

☐ If you are dissatisfied with your financial advisor and are considering leaving.

   YOU CAN'T AFFORD TO STAY IN THE WRONG RELATIONSHIP

Note: Photocopy the checklist before using.

Your Financial Advisor
Is the Relationship Right?

What to Know

Some of the attributes of a good business relationship with a financial advisor include: skillful investment management, sound guidance and advice, a commitment to placing your interests first, good communication, and quality customer service. For many, an alignment of values is also important. When some of these attributes are lacking, it may lead to dissatisfaction.

Is the relationship between you and your advisor right for you? In determining this, some guidance is in order:

☐ Do not evaluate your advisor by cost alone. The value of sound guidance and stewardship within a trust-based relationship is difficult to price.

☐ Do not evaluate your advisor by performance alone, especially over the short-term. The benchmark for performance may be the progress you're making toward meeting your financial goals. Whether or not you "beat the market" may be secondary.

Many insurance agents, brokers and advisers provide financial-related services in addition to investment management. Many are highly-credentialed either by formal education or by professional designation. Their expertise and the services they offer may represent an exceptional value to you. Examples of these services include college, financial and retirement planning, tax-efficient investment strategies, IRA/retirement plan withdrawal strategies, legacy and generational planning, special needs planning, post-divorce planning, and during difficult periods, old-fashioned hand-holding. In most instances, these services are provided to you at no additional cost.

Another way to measure the value of your advisor relationship is client communication and administrative services. There is no excuse for poor or infrequent communication, slow responses to your service requests, sloppy work, frequent mistakes and attitude from receptionists or sales assistants. These alone are grounds for leaving.

The Checklist

Complete the *Assessing the Relationship* checklist on page 80. Your answers to the checklist questions will help you determine whether your financial advisor is Mr. or Ms. "Right". <u>Return to this section after you've completed the checklist.</u>

Reviewing Your Checklist Answers

How is the relationship between you and your advisor? Mostly "yes" answers may indicate a good relationship. Mostly "no" answers may suggest a relationship with gaps between what your needs and preferences are, and what your advisor provides. It may also indicate shortfalls in what you should reasonably expect from a full-service financial advisor.

If your *Relationship Assessment* shows shortfalls or gaps that have you concerned or dissatisfied, use the following sequence of actions with your advisor:

What to Do: Part 1

1. Meet with your advisor and discuss your concerns or dissatisfaction. Your *Relationship Assessment* will be helpful in providing the specifics.

2. Give your advisor the opportunity to resolve the problems to your satisfaction. Be specific with the corrective action you expect from your advisor.

There are other important factors or circumstances that may affect your relationship with your financial advisor:

☐ Conflicting personalities and communication styles can create discomfort and a sense of dissatisfaction with your advisor. Often there is no fix for this.

☐ A change in your financial circumstances, your needs and your preferences can also create a miss-match between you and your financial advisor. Your advisor may not be capable of providing expert advice on financial-related matters beyond investment management. You may simply outgrow your advisor.

☐ If the trust between you and your financial advisor has been broken or drawn into question, it is unlikely that he or she will ever completely regain it. Leaving your advisor is often the only solution.

If the shortfalls or gaps in your *Relationship Assessment* are not corrected to your satisfaction, or if other important factors or circumstances lead you to believe that leaving your financial advisor is your only option, the question is: what do you do next?

What to Do: Part 2

You can't afford to jump out of one relationship and into another. Use the following two guides and checklists before you make any decisions:

☐ Guide: *Financial Advisors: An Overview* p. 54

This guide will help familiarize you with the three basic types of advisors, the products and services they offer, and the standard of care they are held to in the handling of their clients' accounts:

☐ Guide: *Financial Advisors: Finding Mr. or Ms. "Right"* p. 61
Checklist: *Finding Mr. or Ms. "Right",* Part 1 and Part 2   p. 64 and p. 73

This guide will help you determine which type of advisor, which investment products and services, and which standard of care is most appropriate for your financial circumstances, needs and preferences. The guide also provides direction on where you might find Mr. or Ms. "Right". Easy-to-follow instructions are included in the guide.

Note: If you like the firm your financial advisor is with and the office is conveniently located, you may be able to find another advisor within the firm that's more suitable for you. The branch manager can be helpful in finding you another advisor. In this case, everything about your account would stay the same except you'd have a new advisor of record on your account.

Transferring Your Account

Transferring your account to a new financial advisor and a new brokerage/advisory firm is automated. While your former advisor is alerted that your account is transferring, they are not directly involved in the process. Here's how it works:

The financial institution that you are transferring your account to is referred to as the "receiving firm" (your new advisor's firm). The receiving firm initiates the transfer by submitting your signed ACATS form (Automatic Customer Account Transfer System) to the "delivering firm" (your former advisor's firm). This automated transfer process is typically completed within six business days.

Fees are synonymous with financial services. When you transfer your account, the delivering firm typically charges a transfer fee. These charges are generally between $50 and $100. Other fees, like closing an IRA may also apply. As a gesture of appreciation, the receiving firm may credit your account for the transfer fees the delivering firm charged you.

Caution: you may have investments that have back-end sales charges. If your new advisor directs the delivering firm (your old advisor's firm) to sell these investments, or if your new advisor plans to sell them once they transfer over, you may incur substantial charges. Make sure you're on top of this. Get justifications for any recommended sales.

While leaving your financial advisor may be difficult, *your interests must come first.* Forming the right relationship with the right advisor offers tremendous long-term value for you. You can't afford to stay in a relationship that isn't right.

Assessing the Relationship
Is The Relationship Right?

Client Service and Communication

Does your financial advisor or the sales assistant return your calls within a timeframe that's acceptable to you?

☐ Yes ☐ No ☐ Most of the time ☐ Some of the time

Does your advisor's sales assistant address you professionally and courteously?

☐ Yes ☐ No ☐ Most of the time ☐ Some of the time

Is the receptionist professional and courteous?

☐ Yes ☐ No ☐ Most of the time ☐ Some of the time

Are your service requests handled quickly, thoroughly, and accurately?

☐ Yes ☐ No ☐ Most of the time ☐ Some of the time

If mistakes occur, is your advisor or the sales assistant quick to take responsibility and correct the mistake?

☐ Yes ☐ No ☐ Most of the time ☐ Some of the time

Your Financial Advisor

Service

Do you receive periodic, "just checking in" service calls from your advisor that are NOT tied to an investment recommendation or sales pitch?

☐ Yes ☐ No ☐ Most of the time ☐ Some of the time

Does your advisor listen intently to your questions and concerns? Is he or she earnestly engaged during phone conversations?

☐ Yes ☐ No ☐ Most of the time ☐ Some of the time

Does your advisor give you complete answers to your questions, and provide explanations that are understandable and to your level of satisfaction?

☐ Yes ☐ No ☐ Most of the time ☐ Some of the time

Does your advisor offer non-commercial educational seminars, provide periodic reports or newsletters on important financial-related topics?

☐ Yes ☐ No

Investment Management

Do you understand the investments you own and the activity in your account to your level of satisfaction?

☐ Yes ☐ No

Does your advisor periodically provide a performance report that compares the performance of your account against an appropriate benchmark?

☐ Yes ☐ No ☐ Not sure

Does your advisor periodically disclose all commissions, fees and other underlying expenses associated with your account?

☐ Yes ☐ No ☐ Not sure

Does your advisor periodically calculate your personal net worth?

☐ Yes ☐ No ☐ Not sure

Other Services

Does your advisor provide you with other financial-related services beyond investment management? For example, financial, insurance and legacy planning, or specialized services and advice on family-related matters like special needs, aging parents, and post-divorce planning?

☐ Yes ☐ No ☐ Not sure

In providing those services, would he or she be acting as an expert?

☐ Yes ☐ No ☐ Not sure

Does you advisor actively engage other experts and allied professionals to the benefit of your account? For example, your attorney, CPA/accountant, or financial advisors with specific areas of expertise?

☐ Yes ☐ No ☐ Not sure

Personal

Are you able to discuss personal or family-related matters with your advisor?

☐ Yes ☐ No ☐ Not sure

Does your advisor counsel you against making emotional decisions?

☐ Yes ☐ No ☐ Most of the time ☐ Some of the time

Does he or she help you manage your emotions and behavior in a manner that elevates the probability of you achieving your long-term investment related goals?

☐ Yes ☐ No ☐ Most of the time ☐ Some of the time

Are you comfortable with your advisor? Do your personalities mix well?

☐ Yes ☐ No

Are your personal values aligned with your advisor's?

☐ Yes ☐ No ☐ Not sure

Is this important to you?

☐ Yes ☐ No

Conflicts of Interests

Does your advisor put you first in the relationship and place your interests ahead of his or her interests or those of their company?

☐ Yes ☐ No ☐ Not sure

Return to **"Reviewing Your Checklist Answers"** on page 77 of this guide.

Your New Investment Account

Okay, What's the Plan?

Checklist

My New Investment Account: What's the Plan? p. 87

How Long Does it Take to Do?

About 20 minutes. Your financial advisor provides all the information.

When to Use

☐ Use this guide when you are opening a new investment account. The checklist provides a way for your financial advisor to explain how he or she plans to invest your money, what the cost to do that might be, and the types of investments that may be used in managing your account.

KNOW WHAT YOU'RE GETTING INTO. YOU CAN'T AFFORD TO BE IN THE DARK

Types of Accounts This Guide Applies to

☐ Large and small commission-based accounts

☐ Large and small fee-based advisory accounts

Notes

☐ If you <u>are not</u> already working with the financial advisor, use the following two guides <u>first</u>:

   ☐ Guide: *Financial Advisors: An Overview* p. 54

   ☐ Guide: *Financial Advisors: Finding Mr. or Ms. "Right"* p. 61
   Checklist: *Finding Mr. or Ms. "Right"*, Part 1 & Part 2 p. 64 and p. 73

KNOW WHO YOU'RE WORKING WITH. YOU CAN'T AFFORD TO GET INTO THE WRONG RELATIONSHIP

☐ Photocopy the checklist before using.

Your New Investment Account: Okay, What's the Plan?

Dear advisor: just a few questions...

Instructions

Using the checklist:

☐ READ THROUGH THE CHECKLIST INSTRUCTIONS BEFORE USING

☐ Use during a meeting or phone call with your financial advisor. Your advisor provides all the information to complete the checklist. You fill in the answers.

☐ For question 1, have your advisor answer use key phrases.

☐ Repeat what you've written back to your advisor.

☐ Financial advisors have a regulatory obligation to answer your questions to your level of satisfaction. You can't afford a fuzzy understanding of what's going on with your money!

What do I say to my advisor?

Using your own words, here's what you want to convey: *"To help me better understand how you plan to invest my account, I'd appreciate it if you'd answer the questions I have on my checklist. Your willingness to do this goes a long way in showing me that I come first in our relationship, and that the trust and confidence I'm placing in you is well-founded."*

Notes:

☐ While your financial advisor will have agreements, contracts and disclosures that communicate much of the information your checklist requests,

- only your checklists promote and protect your interests with a set of questions from your side of the relationship,

- only your checklists equip you with questions that apply specifically to the decisions and actions of your financial advisor,

- only your checklists help you evaluate the intent of your financial advisor, and the quality and professionalism of your advisor, by how your questions are answered,

- only your checklists allow you to record and file your financial advisor's direct responses to your questions.

☐ The checklist questions are based on industry "best practices" for disclosure. There are no "zinger" or "gotcha" questions.

☐ Beware of evasive answers or claims that it's "against company policy" to answer.

After completion:

☐ Review for accuracy and completeness with your financial advisor.

☐ File the completed checklist in your *My Best Interests* folder.

The Checklist
The Importance of the Questions

Let's go over the questions on the checklist:

1. Will you put me first in our relationship, and not advance your interests or those of your company at my expense?

 This is the most important question on the checklist. It sets the terms on how your relationship with your advisor is going to work.

Note: With every recommendation and every action, your financial advisor makes a conscious decision to either put you first, or their own interests first. <u>News Flash: regulations and "standard of care" rules do not guide this decision.</u> It's guided by personal integrity, or by the absence of this trait.

? What does a good answer look like?

A direct "yes" is the only acceptable answer. You can't afford to enter into a relationship with a financial advisor who won't put you first.

2. How do you plan on investing my account?

Waiting to be surprised on how your account is going to be invested isn't good business. You need to know what your financial advisor plans to do with your money before you invest a penny.

? What does a good answer look like?

<u>It doesn't need to be a complicated answer.</u> All you're looking for is a brief explanation of what your advisor's strategy is for your account, and the types of investments he or she might consider using. That's it. Your advisor has a regulatory obligation to make sure you understand their answer.

Note: If your advisor is recommending an annuity, he or she must also complete the appropriate *Buying an Annuity* checklist before you make a decision. No excuses. If your account is commission-based, and your advisor is recommending mutual funds, he or she must also complete the *Buying a Mutual Fund* checklist for each fund being recommended. This does not apply to fee-based accounts.

3. How will you receive compensation for the handling of my account?

Depending on whether your account is commission-based, fee-based or fee-only, your financial advisor can receive compensation in different ways. For example, if your account is commission-based, your advisor may receive compensation from items "A" through "E" (see checklist on page 87). If your advisor is also licensed to sell insurance products, he or she may also receive compensation for item "F". If your account is fee-based, your advisor will typically receive item "G" compensation. If your advisor is also licensed to sell insurance products, he or she may also receive compensation through item "F".

? What does a good answer look like?

You expect your advisor to disclose all potential sources of compensation. Confirm with your advisor that all applicable boxes are checked. If your account is going to be fee-based or fee-only, you expect the applicable percentage (if the advisory fee is a percentage of the assets under management), hourly rate, or terms to be disclosed.

4. What is the estimated total cost to initially invest my account stated as a dollar amount and as a percentage of my expected opening account value?

If your account is commission-based, up-front sales charges and other costs can add up during the initial investing phase.

? What does a good answer look like?

You don't need (and shouldn't expect) a to-the-penny accounting of these costs. All you're really looking for is a good faith estimate of what those initial costs may be.

If your advisor plans on using a fee-based "managed" platform/program for your account, you want to know what the advisory fee will be and the payment terms. For example, a fee based upon the size of the account, an hourly rate, flat fee, etc.

5. What is the estimated total cost to manage my account on an annual basis? Please state as a dollar amount range and as a percentage range based upon my expected opening account value.

? What does a good answer look like?

Both the dollar amount and percentage estimates are filled in. This range should also include any mutual fund/ETF internal expenses and mark-up/mark-downs associated with the management of your account. Refer to Quick Course: *Calculating Total Costs,* p. 133, for more information.

Special Note: Your relationship with your financial advisor should be one of your most important and valuable professional relationships. Your checklist allows you to gauge the quality of this relationship by how your advisor answers your questions. Your checklist also allows you to confirm that your advisor puts you first, and that the relationship is based upon openness, fair play and accountability. <u>You can't afford a relationship that doesn't work this way</u>.

My New Investment Account: What's the Plan?

Dear advisor: just a few questions...

Date: _____

1. Will you put me first in our relationship, and not advance your interests or those of your company at my expense?

   ☐ Yes ☐ No

2. How do you plan on investing my account? Please use key phrases.

   _____

   _____

   _____

   _____

   _____

   Types of investments you may consider using: (Check all that apply)

   ☐ Individual stocks, ETFs, etc.

   ☐ Individual bonds

   ☐ Mutual funds

   ☐ Annuities and other insurance-related products

   ☐ Fee-based "managed" account

   ☐ Other: _____

3. How will you receive compensation for handling my account? (Check all that may apply)

   ☐ A: Commissions from buying and selling of individual stocks, ETFs, etc.

   ☐ B: Mark-ups and mark-downs from buying and selling of individual bonds

   ☐ C: Commissions/up-front sales charges on the purchase of mutual funds

   ☐ D: Sales concessions from new securities offerings

   ☐ E: "Trailer"/service fees on mutual funds (typically between 0.25% and 1.00%)

   ☐ F: Commissions on the purchase of annuities and other insurance-related products

   ☐ G: Advisory fee as a percentage of assets under management: _____%

   ☐ H: Hourly rate for advisory services: Rate: $_____ an hour

   ☐ I: Retainer for advisory services: Terms: _____

   ☐ Other: _____

87

Notes: _____

_____

_____

4. What is the estimated total cost to initially invest my account stated as a dollar amount and as a percentage of my expected opening account value?

$ _____ or _____ % of account value

5. What is the estimated total cost to manage my account on an annual basis? Please state as a dollar amount range and as a percentage range based upon my expected opening account value.

Between $ _____ and $ _____ / Between _____ % and _____ %

Your Investments

Know What You Own and Why You Own It

Checklist

My Investments p. 96

How Long Does it Take to Do?

About 15 minutes to review. Your financial advisor provides all the information.

Applies To

☐ All commission-based accounts.

☐ Fee-based accounts in which your financial advisor <u>acts as the investment manager</u>. (Don't know? Just ask your financial advisor.)

When to Use

The purpose of the checklist in this guide is to provide a way for your financial advisor to explain what's going on in your account, and why.

☐ Use the checklist to confirm that your account's asset allocation, how it's diversified, and the individual investments you own are appropriate for you.

☐ Use the checklist annually. If you like more frequent reports, use quarterly.

KNOW WHAT'S GOING ON IN YOUR ACCOUNT. YOU CAN'T AFFORD TO BE IN THE DARK

Note: Photocopy the checklist before using.

Your Investments: for all commission-based accounts, and fee-based accounts in which your financial advisor acts as the money manager

Dear advisor: just a few questions...

Instructions

The Checklist Applies to:

☐ All commission-based accounts

If your account is commission-based, the *My Investments* checklist applies. In commission-based accounts, the financial advisor is usually <u>directly involved</u> in setting the asset allocation for the account, diversifying within the asset classes, and selecting the individual investments.

☐ All fee-based Accounts in which your financial advisor acts as the investment manager

If your account is fee-based and your advisor acts as the investment manager and is <u>directly responsible</u> for setting the asset allocation for your account, diversifying within the asset classes, and selecting the individual investments, the *My Investments* checklist applies. If you don't know if your advisor is acting as the investment manager, just ask.

The Checklist does NOT apply to:

☐ Commission-based accounts with a single investment

If your advisor has you invested in a single mutual fund, the *My Investments* checklist does not apply. In this case, your advisor is <u>not directly involved</u> in asset allocation, diversification or investment selection decisions. The mutual fund manager is. Your advisor's responsibility is limited to selecting a mutual fund that is appropriate for you. Use the *Buying a Mutual Fund* checklist in this situation.

☐ Fee-based mutual fund wrap accounts and fee-based separately managed accounts (SMA)

If your advisor has you invested in a mutual fund advisory account and is using a model portfolio (a preset allocation of mutual funds), or has you in a SMA, the *My Investments* checklist does not apply. In this case, your advisor is <u>not directly involved</u> in asset allocation, diversification or investment selection decisions. In this case, your advisor has delegated that responsibility. Your advisor's responsibility is to monitor the portfolio and provide you with periodic reports. In this situation, use the *Account Returns* and the *Total Costs for Fee-based Accounts* checklists.

Using the checklist:

☐ READ THROUGH THE CHECKLIST INSTRUCTIONS BEFORE USING

☐ Use during a meeting or phone call with your financial advisor. Your advisor provides all the information to complete the checklist. You fill in the answers.

☐ For questions 1, 2 and 3, have your advisor answer using key phrases.

☐ Repeat what you've written back to your advisor.

☐ Your advisor has a regulatory obligation to answer your questions to your level of satisfaction. You can't afford a fuzzy understanding of what's going on with your money!

What do I say to my advisor?

Using your own words, here's what you want to convey: *"To help me better understand the investments I own, and why I own them, I'd appreciate it if you'd answer the questions I have on my checklist. Your willingness to do this goes a long way in showing me that I come first in our relationship, and that the trust and confidence I've placed in you is well-founded."*

Notes:

☐ While your financial advisor may provide you with statements and reports that contain much of the information your checklist requests,

- only your checklists promote <u>and protect your interests</u> with a set of questions from <u>your side</u> of the relationship,

- only your checklists equip you with questions that <u>apply specifically</u> to the decisions and actions of your financial advisor,

- only your checklists help you evaluate the <u>intent</u> of your financial advisor, and the <u>quality and professionalism</u> of your advisor, by how your questions are answered,

- only your checklists allow you to <u>record and file</u> your financial advisor's direct responses to your questions.

☐ The checklist questions are based on industry "best practices" for disclosure. There are no "zinger" or "gotcha" questions.

☐ Beware of evasive answers or claims that it's "against company policy" to answer.

After completion:

☐ Review for accuracy and completeness with your financial advisor.

☐ File the completed checklist in your *My Best Interests* folder.

Your Financial Advisor

Your financial advisor is an expert who is educated, trained and licensed to provide you with investment management services. In this business arrangement, the burden to know and apply difficult investing concepts is off your shoulders and onto your advisor's. But you still need a way to periodically confirm as a consumer – not as a whiz kid – that your account is being managed appropriately. Completing the checklist with your advisor does this. It also shows that you come first in the relationship.

Let's go over the questions on the checklist:

1. **"How is my account allocated to stocks, bonds, cash and other asset classes?"**

   " Asset allocation? I've been told I need to know about this, but my heart just isn't in it to learn."

   " You don't need to know all about asset allocation. All you need are a few smart questions that allow you to confirm that your financial advisor knows all about asset allocation, and is applying it skillfully and appropriately to your account."

   "To help you grasp the basics of asset allocation, let's use a tasty example:"

The Chicken Pot Pie

Your financial advisor plans-out what investments go into your account much like a dietitian would plan a well-balanced meal. And as a dietitian would need to know certain things about your health and dietary needs to plan the right meal, your advisor also needs to know certain things about you. In general, these are: your investment goal, how much time you have to reach your goal, and your stomach for the ups and downs of the market. But instead of portioning different food types onto your plate, your advisor allocates different investment types into your account.

If a dietitian determines you need 68% in complex carbohydrates, 29% in protein and 3% in fat, this may be satisfied with a chicken pot pie. But remember, it's not the chicken pot pie you need, it's what's in it: the right measurements of the right ingredients:

1/3 cup of butter or margarine
1/3 cup chopped onion
1/3 cup all-purpose flour
1/2 teaspoon salt
1/4 teaspoon pepper

1 3/4 cups chicken broth
1/2 cup milk
2 1/2 cups shredded chicken or turkey
2 cups frozen mixed vegetables thawed

So if your advisor determines you need 68% in stocks, 29% in bonds and 3% in cash, what might that "pot pie" of investments look like? Here's an example recipe:

20% Large US Value Stocks
20% Large US Growth Stocks
16% Investment Grade US Bonds
14% Large Non-US Stocks
5% Non-US Investment Grade Bonds
6% Emerging Economy Stocks

4% Emerging Economy Bonds
4% US High Yield Bonds
4% Small US Value Stocks
4% Small US Growth Stocks
3% Money Market Fund

Note: While the dietitian's pot pie may be tasty to everybody, the investment "pot pie" may not be appropriate for all investors. The recipe is provided for educational purposes only and does not represent investment advice.

? Okay… so what does a good answer to question #1 on asset allocation look like?

The allocation percentages are filled in and your advisor has explained why your account is allocated the way it is. This doesn't need to be complicated. A few key phrases are all you need.

Your Financial Advisor

There is no "silver bullet" in asset allocation. Preferences and methodologies differ between advisors as does the manner in which they address their client's financial needs and objectives. This is why it's important for you know what's going on in your account, and understand the thinking behind your advisor's decisions. Your advisor welcomes every opportunity to explain this to you. Their explanations don't need to be long-winded or complicated, either. It's your responsibility to pay attention!

2. **"Explain how my account is diversified within each asset class and why."**

" *I need to know about this too?"*

" *Yep. This doesn't need to get complicated. A few key phrases are all you need."*

Note on Diversification

☐ Diversification is the risk management process of selecting several different investments for each asset class. For example, for the asset class "stocks", owning large company stocks, small company stocks and non-U.S. stocks. In the "pot pie" example, the "vegetable" part of the recipe is diversified among carrots, peas, green beans and corn.

☐ While diversification keeps you from making a killing from owning only one or two "hot" investments, broad diversification protects you from getting killed when the market clobbers them.

For more information, refer to Quick Course: *Asset Allocation*, p. 123, and Quick Course: *Example Investments Categorized by Goal Time Horizon*, p. 125.

? Okay... so what does a good answer to question #2 on diversification look like?

It doesn't have to be a lengthy or technical explanation; just an answer you understand and are satisfied with. Your advisor can explain how your account is diversified and why in about 5 minutes. All you need are a few key phrases you can write down.

3. **"Explain the purpose of each of my individual investments and how each one fits in with the others."**

? *Are you kidding me?...* Okay, what does a good answer look like?

This doesn't need to be overwhelming. It's up to you to decide whether you want highly-detailed explanations or general summarizations about the investments in your account. With preparation, your advisor can explain your investments to you in about 10 minutes. All you need are a few key phrases you can write down.

Helpful Tip

If your account has 10 or fewer investments, your advisor can go over them individually with you. If you have more than 10 investments in your account, an acceptable alternative is to have your advisor group your investments. For example, grouping individual large cap stocks with large cap mutual funds, or grouping high-quality individual bonds with high-quality corporate bond mutual funds. Your advisor can then explain the purpose of each grouping and how it fits in with the other groupings. This will keep things from getting too complicated, and the explanations too lengthy. All you want to know is what you own, and why you own it.

Your Financial Advisor

How your financial advisor diversifies your account selects investments, is based upon their preferences for certain types of investments, management styles and other criteria or indicators. Since your advisor is the "expert" and not you, most of the investment decisions your advisor makes you'll take on faith, knowing your advisor is obligated to do what's right for you. That's the business arrangement.

Your advisor welcomes every opportunity to explain their process for selecting investments for your account. It also provides a way for your advisor to show that you come first in the relationship. It is your responsibility to pay attention! Don't wave-away or cut short their explanations.

Note: In the handling of your account, your financial advisor has a duty of care and loyalty. There are two standards of care that apply to financial advisors: the "suitability" standard and the "fiduciary" standard. The "suitability" standard of care applies to commission-based accounts, and the "fiduciary" standard applies to fee-based advisory accounts. Consequently, question 4 is asked differently depending on the type of account you have.

If Your Account is Commission-Based:

4. Are my account's asset allocation, level of diversification, and individual investments all suitable for me?

 Note: It is the most important question on the checklist.
There are two versions of this question: one for commission-based accounts, and one for fee-based accounts.

Most of us expect our financial advisor to do what's right for us. "Doing what's right" is intuitive. We don't need legal definitions to know what it means and the intent behind it. But there is one regulatory term you need to know about: "suitability".

" *Suitability?"*

> **"** *Suitability" is regulatory-speak for "doing what's right". Your advisor has a <u>regulatory obligation</u> to have a reasonable basis for believing that your account's allocation, level of diversification and individual investments are suitable or "right" for your needs, financial situation, investment objective, risk tolerance, etc."*

? What does a good answer look like?
A direct "yes" is the only acceptable answer.

If Your Account is Fee-Based (applicable accounts):

4. Are my account's asset allocation, level of diversification, and individual investments all in my best interests?

If your account is a fee-based advisory account and your advisor acts as the investment manager and is <u>directly responsible</u> for setting the asset allocation for your account, diversifying, and selecting the individual investments, your advisor has a duty to take special care in managing your account. Your account's allocation, level of diversification and individual investments must all be in your best interests.

" *Best interests?*
What does that mean?"

> **"** *It means your advisor has a <u>fiduciary obligation</u> to allocate, diversify and select investments for your account in a way that is <u>most advantageous and beneficial</u> in light of your circumstances, financial situation, investment objective, risk tolerance, etc. These decisions and recommendations must also be made without regard to the financial interests or other interests of your advisor."*

? What does a good answer look like?
A direct "yes" is the only acceptable answer.

Special Note: Your relationship with your financial advisor should be one of your most important and valuable professional relationships. Your checklist allows you to gauge the quality of this relationship by how your advisor answers your questions. Your checklist also allows you to confirm that your advisor puts you first, and that the relationship is based upon openness, fair play and accountability. <u>You can't afford a relationship that doesn't work this way</u>.

My Investments

Dear advisor: just a few questions...

Date: _____

Title of account: _____

Firm: _____ Account number: _____

For the reporting period: _____ to _____

1. How is my account allocated to stocks, bonds, cash and other asset classes and why?

   Asset Allocation: Stocks: _____% Bonds: _____% Cash: _____% Other: _____%

   Notes: _____

   _____

2. Explain how my account is diversified within each asset class and why.

   Key phrases: _____

   _____

   _____

   _____

3. Explain the purpose of each of my individual investments (or groupings) and how each one fits in with the others. (Use an additional sheet if necessary).

   Key phrases: _____

   _____

   _____

   _____

   _____

   Commission-based Account:
4. Are my account's asset allocation, level of diversification, and individual investments all suitable for me?

   ☐ Confirmed "yes" by my advisor

   Fee-based Account (applicable accounts):
   Are my account's asset allocation, level of diversification, and individual investments all in my best interests?

   ☐ Confirmed "yes" by my advisor

Trading Activity

For Commission-based Accounts

Checklist

Trading Activity p. 101

How Long Does it Take to Do?

About 15 minutes. Your financial advisor provides all the information.

When to Use

☐ The checklist provides a way for your financial advisor to confirm that all trades in your account were appropriate and authorized by you.

KNOW WHAT'S GOING ON IN YOUR ACCOUNT. YOU CAN'T AFFORD TO BE IN THE DARK

☐ Use the checklist quarterly. If there's a lot of trading activity, use monthly.

Note: Photocopy the checklist before using.

Trading Activity: Commission-based Accounts
Dear advisor: just a few questions...

Instructions

Using the checklist:

☐ READ THROUGH THE CHECKLIST INSTRUCTIONS BEFORE USING

☐ Use during a meeting or phone call with your financial advisor. Your advisor provides all the information to complete the checklist. You fill in the answers.

☐ Repeat what you've written back to your advisor.

☐ Your financial advisor has a regulatory obligation to answer your questions to your level of satisfaction. You can't afford a fuzzy understanding of what's going on with your money!

What do I say to my advisor?

Using your own words, here's what you want to convey: *"To help me better understand the trading activity in my account, I'd appreciate it if you'd answer the questions I have on my checklist. Your willingness to do this goes a long way in showing me that I come first in our relationship, and that the trust and confidence I've placed in you is well-founded."*

Notes:

☐ While your advisor's brokerage/advisory firm formally communicates all trading activity to you through trade confirmations,

- only your checklists promote and protect your interests with a set of questions from your side of the relationship,

- only your checklists equip you with questions that apply specifically to the decisions and actions of your financial advisor,

- only your checklists help you evaluate the intent of your financial advisor, and the quality and professionalism of your advisor, by how your questions are answered,

- only your checklists allow you to record and file your financial advisor's direct responses to your questions.

☐ The checklist questions are based on industry "best practices" for disclosure. There are no "zinger" or "gotcha" questions.

☐ Beware of evasive answers or claims that it's "against company policy" to answer.

After completion:

☐ Review for accuracy and completeness with your financial advisor.

☐ File the completed checklist in your *My Best Interests* folder.

The Checklist
The Importance of the Questions

Before any buy or sell can take place in your account, your commission-based advisor has a regulatory requirement to get your approval before executing the trade. This type of account is known as a "non-discretionary" account. This is why registered reps or "brokers" are always on the phone with their customers making buy and sell recommendations and confirming approval for each transaction.

Your Financial Advisor

Your financial advisor welcomes the opportunity to explain the trades in your account. This checklist also allows your advisor to show evidence that you come first in the relationship. Trades that aren't excessive or costly are a good way to show that.

Let's go over the questions on the checklist:

Start the checklist by filling-in your account information.

1. **Confirm whether there were new "buys" and/or "sells" during the period.**

    Your advisor can confirm this or you can yourself by reviewing the "Account Activity" section in your brokerage account statement(s). If there were no new buys or sells during the period, check the box and file the checklist.

     Most of us expect our financial advisor to do what's right for us. "Doing what's right" is intuitive. We don't need legal definitions to know what it means and the intentions behind it. But there is one regulatory term you need to know about: "suitability".

    ❝ Suitability?"

    > *❝ Suitability is regulatory-speak for "doing what's right". Your advisor has a <u>regulatory obligation</u> to only make trades in your account that he or she believes to be suitable or "right" for your needs, financial situation, investment objective, risk tolerance, etc. The next question is about suitability:"*

2. **Was each new buy suitable for my account?**

    This question allows your financial advisor to confirm that each new buy in your account was suitable. .

    ? What does a good answer look like?
    A direct "yes" is the only acceptable answer.

3. **Was the number of new buys suitable for me?**

    This question allows your financial advisor to confirm that the number of new trades in your account was suitable and not excessive.

? What does a good answer look like?

A direct "yes" is the only acceptable answer.

The last two questions on the checklist pertain to "sells" in your account. As with "buys", each individual sell must be suitable, and the number of sells must not be excessive.

? What do good answers look like?

A direct "yes" to each question is the only acceptable answer.

Note on Trading Activity

Trading activity in your account is closely monitored by your financial advisor's firm. While this minimizes the potential for inappropriate activity and excessive commissions, it's important for you to stay on top of what's going on.

How much trading is too much? That depends. An account with an "Aggressive Growth" investment objective may have more frequent trading activity that may involve different types of investments than an account with a "Moderate Growth and Income" investment objective. It's on your advisor to confirm suitability.

For additional information on trading activity and trade confirmations, refer to Quick Course: *Your Account Documents,* p. 136.

Special Note: Your relationship with your financial advisor should be one of your most important and valuable professional relationships. Your checklist allows you to gauge the quality of this relationship by how your advisor answers your questions. Your checklist also allows you to confirm that your advisor puts you first, and that the relationship is based upon openness, fair play and accountability. <u>You can't afford a relationship that doesn't work this way</u>.

Trading Activity: Commission-based Accounts
Dear advisor: just a few questions...

Date: _____

Title of account: _____

Firm: _____ Account number: _____

For the reporting period: _____ to _____

No new buys or sells for the reporting period.

☐ Confirmed by me or my advisor

Note: If there was no trading activity for the reporting period, check the box and file the checklist.

Buys
Was each new buy suitable for my account?

☐ Confirmed "yes" by my advisor

Was the number of new buys in my account suitable for me?

☐ Confirmed "yes" by my advisor

Sells
Was each investment sold suitable for my account?

☐ Confirmed "yes" by my advisor

Was the number of sells in my account suitable for me?

☐ Confirmed "yes" by my advisor

Account Returns

Know How You're Doing and Compared to What

Checklist

My Account's Return p. 108

How Long Does it Take to Do?

About 15 minutes. Your financial advisor provides all the information.

When to Use

☐ When you want to know the rate of return on your account, and whether the return was good, or not-so-good, when compared to a standard or "benchmark".

NOT KNOWING HOW YOUR ACCOUNT IS DOING COULD BE COSTING YOU HUNDREDS OR EVEN THOUSANDS OF DOLLARS A YEAR

IF YOU DON'T COMPARE YOUR ACCOUNT'S RETURN TO A BENCHMARK, YOU HAVE NO WAY OF KNOWING WHETHER YOUR FINANCIAL ADVISOR IS ADDING ANY VALUE. THAT'S NOT GOOD BUSINESS.

Applies To

☐ Large and small commission-based accounts

☐ Large and small fee-based advisory accounts

☐ Accounts with only investment. For example, a mutual fund

Notes

☐ Use the checklist annually. If you like more frequent reports, use quarterly.

☐ Photocopy the checklist before using.

Account Returns
Dear advisor: just a few questions...

Instructions

Using the checklist:

- [ ] READ THROUGH THE CHECKLIST INSTRUCTIONS BEFORE USING

- [ ] The best way to use this checklist is during a meeting with your financial advisor. Your advisor provides all the information to complete the checklist. You fill in the answers.

- [ ] Repeat what you've written back to your advisor.

- [ ] You can also complete the checklist during a phone call with your financial advisor. Repeat what you've written back to your advisor.

What do I say to my advisor?

Using your own words, here's what you want to convey: *"To help me better understand how my account is doing, I'd appreciate it if you'd answer the questions I have on my checklist. Your willingness to do this goes a long way in showing me that I come first in our relationship, and that the trust and confidence I've placed in you is well-founded."*

Notes:

- [ ] Your financial advisor may be prohibited by company policy from calculating a benchmark return to compare your account's return against. To get this vital piece of information, a workaround that you can do yourself is provided in this guide.

- [ ] If your account is fee-based, you may receive reports that show your account's return compared against a benchmark. While these reports provide valuable information, <u>only your checklist promotes and protects your interests with a set of questions from your side of the relationship, and only your checklist allows you to record and file your financial advisor's direct responses to those questions.</u>

- [ ] The checklist questions are based on industry "best practices" for disclosure. There are no "zinger" or "gotcha" questions.

After completion:

- [ ] Review for accuracy and completeness with your financial advisor.

- [ ] File the completed checklist in your *My Best Interests* folder.

The Checklist
The Importance of the Questions

Saying your account "did pretty well" or was "down just a little" is a very loose way of evaluating how your investments are doing. A better way is to have your financial advisor answer two important questions about your account: "how is it doing?" and "compared to what?" Bottom line: not knowing the answer to this two-part question could be costing you hundreds or even thousands of dollars every year.

Let's go over the questions on the checklist:

Start the checklist by filling-in your account information and the reporting period.

1. **Have your advisor provide the data to fill in Part 1.**

    ? What does a good answer look like?

    ☐ It includes the rate of return

    Note: Getting your account's rate of return is easy. Most full-service financial advisors are able to generate "on demand" performance reports right from their computer, and most brokerage/advisory firms offer enhanced statements that include your account's rate of return for the stated reporting period.

    ☐ The return applies to a stated time period e.g., quarter, full-year, etc.

    ☐ The "yes" box on the net of fees/costs is checked

    Note: If you have a commission-based account, the return is typically stated net of commissions and sales charges. (Any commissions or sales charges you paid are included in the cost basis of each investment you own.)

    If you have a fee-based account, confirm that the return is calculated net of the advisory fee you pay to your advisor. Calculating returns without deducting advisory fees may misrepresent the value being added or subtracted by your advisor.

Your Financial Advisor

Do not evaluate your advisor by performance alone, especially over the short-term. While competitive returns are always important, consistently "beating the market" is nearly impossible. What's always possible is for your advisor to demonstrate that you come first in the relationship. One way to do this is through open and ongoing communication, regardless of whether the news is good, bad, or even ugly. This checklist provides a way for your advisor to periodically report your account's return, and evaluate the return against a benchmark. With this information, your advisor can stay the course, or plan corrective action.

2. Have your advisor provide the benchmark information to fill in Part 2.

" Benchmark?"

> *" That's the "compared to what" part. Knowing the return on your account without knowing whether the return was good - or not so good - isn't very useful.*

Note: <u>If you don't compare your account's return to a standard or "benchmark", you have no way of knowing whether your advisor's investment decisions are adding any value.</u> That's not good business.

To better understand this (without getting into the weeds), let's take a quick course on benchmarks:

Quick Course: Benchmarks

Index
An index tracks the performance of a specific "basket" of stocks, bonds and other types of investments. An index can represent a broad market, a section of a broad market, a region in the world, or a country. There are thousands of indexes. Some of the more popular ones are the S&P 500, the Dow Jones Industrial, and the NASDAQ 100.

Benchmark
A benchmark is a standard. By comparing the return of your account against a benchmark, you can determine whether your account's return was competitive or underperforming. Generally, an index is used as a benchmark.

Setting a Benchmark
<u>Setting a benchmark doesn't have to get complicated.</u>

How does this work? Let's say your account is invested 100% in a large company stock mutual fund. In this example, your advisor may benchmark (measure) your fund's return against a large company stock index like the S&P 500 Index. Now what? We find out whether your investment is pulling its weight! The benchmark's return helps your advisor determine this:

Large co. stock mutual fund return: 8%   Benchmark return: 7%

Now let's say your advisor has 50% of your account invested in a large company stock mutual fund, and the other half of your account invested in a corporate bond mutual fund. In this example, your advisor would construct a "blended" benchmark using more than one index: the 50% you have in the large company stock fund may be benchmarked to the S&P 500 Index, and the 50% you have in a corporate bond fund may be benchmarked to a bond index like the Barclays Capital US Aggregate Bond Index, for example.

Large co. stock mutual fund return: 8%   Benchmark return: 7%
Corporate bond mutual fund return: <u>4%</u>   Benchmark return: <u>3%</u>

Account return (blended return):   6%   Blended Benchmark return: 5%

Let's say the full-year return on your account was 6%. If your blended benchmark (the two your advisor selected) returned only 5% for the year, you'd be having a very different discussion with your advisor than if the benchmark had returned 8%!

? What does a good answer to Part 2 look like?

☐ Your advisor selected a single benchmark (index) or constructs a blended benchmark (more than one index) that represents how your account is invested.

☐ Your advisor calculated the return on that benchmark.

☐ The benchmark return is subtracted from your account's rate of return. Using the above example, 6 - 5 = 1. In this example, your advisor/investments added 1% of extra return over the benchmark's return.

☐ The benchmarks your advisor used and their percentage weighting in the calculation are listed on the checklist.

Note 1: If your financial advisor is prohibited from calculating a benchmark return to compare your account's return against, that's okay. To get this vital piece of information, have your advisor provide you with the benchmarks, their percentage weightings, and their returns for the period. For example,

☐ 50% S&P 500 Index: 4% return

☐ 10% Russell 2000 Small Cap Index: 5% return

☐ 40% Barclays Capital US Aggregate Bond Index: 1% return

With this information you can do the calculations yourself. It only takes a few minutes and the math is easy. Refer to Quick Course: *Calculating Returns,* p. 127, and Quick Course: *Benchmarking Returns,* p. 129.

Note 2: If your account is fee-based, you will typically receive a report that includes your account's return compared against a benchmark. While this report provides valuable information, <u>only your checklist protects your interests with a set of questions from your side of the relationship.</u>

Note 3: If your account contains only one mutual fund, your advisor may elect to provide you with a report through a third-party mutual fund rating/ranking service. These reports typically provide both the mutual fund's return and the fund's benchmark return. <u>This report does not replace your checklist.</u>

If you paid a front-end sales charge (load) when purchasing your mutual fund, the actual performance of <u>your account</u> may be lower than the reported return for the mutual fund. Your advisor welcomes the opportunity to explain this.

Note on Goals-based Benchmarks

You and your advisor may believe that the most important context is you and your goals - not the financial marketplace. In this context, "good performance" is a return that meets or beats your target return and keeps you moving ahead toward your goals, while "poor performance" is a return that has you falling behind. How does an internal benchmark work? Here's an example:

Let's say you and your advisor have determined that you need a 7% average rate of return over the next 20 years to meet your long-term goal. And let's say the S&P 500 Index (the stock market) returned 10% for a given year, and your account returned only 8%. Though you underperformed the stock market by 2%, you outperformed your required rate of return by 1% which keeps you progressing toward your long-term goal.

Many advisors recommend betting on the tortoise to meet your long-term goals, not the hare. Chase your goals not the markets!

3. **Part 3 of the checklist is for goals-based benchmarks. If your advisor uses a goals-based benchmark, complete this part with your advisor.**

? What does a good answer look like?

☐ Your goals-based benchmark is entered. This is generally stated as the minimum annual rate of return you need to meet your goal.

☐ Your goals-based benchmark (minimum acceptable rate of return) is subtracted from your account's return.

☐ Best practices would also compare your account's return against an external (index-based) benchmark.

Note: While measuring account performance in the context of your goals may be your central consideration, we believe it's still important to confirm that your investments are pulling their weight by measuring their returns against an external benchmark.

Special Note: Your relationship with your financial advisor should be one of your most important and valuable professional relationships. Your checklist allows you to gauge the quality of this relationship by how your advisor answers your questions. Your checklist also allows you to confirm that your advisor puts you first, and that the relationship is based upon openness, fair play and accountability. <u>You can't afford a relationship that doesn't work this way</u>.

My Account's Return
Dear advisor: just a few questions...

Date: _____

Title of account:_____

Firm: _____ Account number: _____

For the reporting period: _____ to _____

Part 1

What was the return on my account for the reporting period?   Account Return: _____%

Is the return net of advisory fees/costs?   ☐ Yes ☐ No

Part 2

How did my account's performance compare against
the benchmark or my goals-based benchmark?

Benchmark Return: _____%

Goals-based Target Return: _____%

Excess Return/Shortfall: _____%
(Difference between account return and benchmark return)

Benchmark or blended benchmark and the percentage weighting used:

Benchmark: _____ Percentage: _____%
Benchmark: _____ Percentage: _____%
Benchmark: _____ Percentage: _____%
Benchmark: _____ Percentage: _____%
Benchmark: _____ Percentage: _____%

Part 3

How did the performance of my account compare against my goals-based benchmark?

Goals-based benchmark: ☐ Not applicable

_____

_____

Total Costs: Commission-based Accounts

Know What You're Paying For, and How Much That is

Checklist

Total Costs: Commission-based Accounts p. 113

How Long Does it Take to Do?

About 15 minutes. Your financial advisor provides all the information.

When to Use

☐ Use when you want to know what the total costs are for doing business with your financial advisor. The checklist provides a way for your advisor to itemize the total costs associated with the management of your account.

NOT KNOWING COULD BE COSTING YOU HUNDREDS OR EVEN THOUSANDS OF DOLLARS A YEAR

☐ Use the checklist annually. If you have a lot of trading activity, use quarterly.

Note: Photocopy the checklist before using.

Total Costs: Commission-based Accounts
`Dear advisor: just a few questions...`

Instructions

Using the checklist:

☐ READ THROUGH THE CHECKLIST INSTRUCTIONS BEFORE USING

☐ Use during a meeting or phone call with your financial advisor. Your advisor provides all the information to complete the checklist. You fill in the answers.

☐ Repeat what you've written back to your advisor.

☐ Your financial advisor has a regulatory obligation to answer your questions to your level of satisfaction. You can't afford a fuzzy understanding of what's going on with your money!

What do I say to my advisor?

Using your own words, here's what you want to convey: *"To help me better understand my total costs, I'd appreciate it if you'd answer the questions I have on my checklist. Your willingness to do this goes a long way in showing me that I come first in our relationship, and that the trust and confidence I've placed in you is well-founded."*

Notes:

☐ While your financial advisor may provide you with a report that contains much of the information your checklist requests,

- only your checklists promote <u>and protect your interests</u> with a set of questions from <u>your side </u>of the relationship,

- only your checklists equip you with questions that <u>apply specifically</u> to the decisions and actions of your financial advisor,

- only your checklists help you evaluate the <u>intent</u> of your financial advisor, and the <u>quality and professionalism</u> of your advisor, by how your questions are answered,

- only your checklists allow you to <u>record and file</u> your financial advisor's direct responses to your questions.

☐ The checklist questions are based on industry "best practices" for disclosure. There are no "zinger" or "gotcha" questions.

☐ Beware of evasive answers or claims that it's "against company policy" to answer.

After completion:

☐ Review for accuracy and completeness with your financial advisor.

☐ File the completed checklist in your *My Best Interests* folder.

What to Know

You probably know what you pay for most goods and services, but do you really know what you're paying in commissions and other costs? <u>Excessive commissions and other costs are money out of your pocket!</u> This can add-up to a lot of money over a several-year period. You could be paying out hundreds or even thousands of dollars every year that you'd scream about paying - if you knew.

Your Financial Advisor

Caution: Do not evaluate your advisor by cost alone. The value of sound guidance and stewardship within a trust-based relationship is difficult to price. But while guidance and stewardship are important, they can't be evaluated in isolation. The full context of the relationship must be taken into consideration. This includes the investment management skill and the cost containment efforts of your financial advisor.

Most financial advisors will work with you to establish a mutually agreed-upon commission schedule that takes into consideration the minimum ticket charge (minimum allowable commission set by the brokerage firm) and a commission amount that is set as a percentage of the dollar amount of the trade. For example, a smaller trade of $2,000 may have the minimum ticket charge apply. A $7,500 trade with a commission set at 1% would be $75. A $20,000 trade with a commission set at 0.75% would be $150.

If you own individual bonds, there are transaction charges for each bond you buy or sell. When you buy a bond, the transaction charge is known as a "mark-up" and when you sell a bond it is known as a "mark-down". Your advisor will provide you with the amount you paid in mark-ups for bonds you bought, and what you paid in mark-down for bonds you sold. Your advisor has this information. (Don't worry, it's a line item on the checklist.)

If you have mutual funds or exchange-traded funds (ETF) in your account, there are underlying expenses associated with owning them. Your advisor will calculate the total amount you're paying in underlying expenses. This is easy for your advisor to do and should be expected from a full-service financial advisor. You also need to be aware of any transaction costs associated with the buying or selling of these funds. This is on the checklist, too.

" So just asking my advisor how much I'm paying in commissions may not give me a complete accounting of all the costs and fees that affect my bottom line, right?"

" You got it. Who knows, commissions may not even be your biggest cost!"

Your Financial Advisor

Having your advisor provide you with the total costs of doing business with them goes a long way in showing that you come first in the relationship, and that the trust and confidence you've placed in them is well-founded. Controlling your total costs is a good way to measure that.

The Checklist
The Importance of the Questions

Start the checklist by filling-in your account information and the reporting period.

1. **Your advisor will provide the following information:**
   - ☐ Total commissions for the period.

   - ☐ Total mark-up/mark-downs on bond trades (if applicable) and any built-in concessions on securities offerings (if applicable).

   - ☐ An estimate of the dollar amount you paid during the reporting period in the form of internal expenses on mutual fund/ETFs or other investments (if applicable) using your account's period-closing investments and values.

     Note: These expenses aren't typically talked about or accounted for, but you pay them year after year. Calculating these costs is not difficult or time-consuming for your advisor to do. And while market conditions and additions/subtractions to holdings during the reporting period will affect the actual internal expenses you paid, it does provide a <u>rough snapshot</u> of your costs, while <u>creating an awareness of them</u>.

   - ☐ Total front-end sales charges you paid to buy mutual funds or other investment products that carry a front-end sales charge (if applicable).

2. **Calculate your total costs.**

   You or your advisor will divide the total costs for the period by your account's closing value to get your total costs as a percentage of your account value. Note: <u>This calculation is best used to evaluate full-year costs</u>. The amount you pay in total costs can vary significantly from one quarter to another. Investing new funds deposited into your account, selling investments to raise cash for a withdrawal, or a change in strategy can significantly increase your costs during the reporting period in which they occur.

? How do I know whether the checklist is completed properly?

Every field is filled and the total costs are calculated.

What Are Acceptable Costs?

It depends on your investment objective. If you have an "Aggressive Growth" investment objective, and you're okay with trading stocks on a frequent basis, you may have higher total costs than if your investment objective is "Moderate Growth and Income" and you prefer to buy and hold your investments. Also, some types of investments are generally more expensive than others. For example, an emerging markets mutual fund is generally more expensive than a domestic large company stock mutual fund. Why? Because researching companies in far-away places with not a lot of published research on them is more expensive than researching domestic large companies with lots of available information on them.

Trading activity and commissions generated from your account are closely monitored by your advisor's firm. While this minimizes the potential for inappropriate activity and excessive commissions, it's important for you to stay on top of what's going on in your account. Using this checklist in combination with the *Trading Activity* guide and Quick Course: *Calculating Total Costs,* p. 133, will help you determine whether the costs are acceptable to you. If they are not, have a talk with your advisor. Most advisor are willing to accommodate reasonable requests for cost reductions.

Total Costs: Commission-based Accounts
Dear advisor: just a few questions...

Date: _____

Title of account: _____

Firm: _____ Account number: _____

Reporting period: _____ to _____

Opening Account Value: $_____ Closing Account Value: $_____

Commissions paid for stock/ETF, etc. transactions for the period[1]: $_____

Mark-ups and mark-downs/concessions: $_____

Estimated dollar amount paid during the reporting period in internal expenses on mutual funds/ETFs, etc. (if applicable) using period-closing investments and values[2]: $_____

Front-end/back-end sales charges on mutual funds/other products: $_____

Total Costs: $_____

Total Cost Calculation
Total estimated costs stated as a percentage of your account value[1]:

Total Costs $_____ / Closing Account Value $_____ = _____%

Note: While you can use this calculation quarterly or semi-annually, it is best used to evaluate full-year costs.

[1] The amount you pay in commissions, mark-up/mark-downs, and front-end sales charges can vary significantly from one reporting period to another. For example, investing new funds deposited into your account, selling investments to raise cash for a withdrawal, and a change in investment strategy can significantly increase your costs during the reporting period in which they occur.

[2] Calculating these costs is not difficult or time-consuming for your advisor to do. While market conditions and additions/ subtractions to holdings during the reporting period will affect the actual internal expenses you paid, it does provide a rough estimate of what you may be paying in internal expenses on mutual funds, ETFs and other products in your account.

Total Costs: Fee-based Accounts

Know What You're Paying For, and How Much That is

Checklist

Total Costs: Fee-based Accounts p. 118

How Long Does it Take to Do?

About 15 minutes. Your financial advisor provides all the information.

When to Use

☐ Use when you want to know what the total costs are for doing business with your financial advisor. The checklist provides a way for your advisor to itemize the total costs associated with the management of your account.

NOT KNOWING COULD BE COSTING YOU HUNDREDS OR EVEN THOUSANDS OF DOLLARS A YEAR

☐ Use the checklist annually.

Note: Photocopy the checklist before using.

Total Costs: Fee-based Accounts
Dear advisor: just a few questions...

Instructions

Using the checklist:

☐ READ THROUGH THE CHECKLIST INSTRUCTIONS BEFORE USING

☐ Use during a meeting with your financial advisor. Your advisor provides all the information to complete the checklist. You fill in the answers.

☐ Repeat what you've written back to your advisor.

☐ Your financial advisor has a regulatory obligation to answer your questions to your level of satisfaction. You can't afford a fuzzy understanding of what's going on with your money!

What do I say to my advisor?

Using your own words, here's what you want to convey: *"To help me better understand my total costs, I'd appreciate it if you'd answer the questions I have on my checklist. Your willingness to do this goes a long way in showing me that I come first in our relationship, and that the trust and confidence I've placed in you is well-founded."*

Notes:

☐ While your financial advisor may provide you with a report that contains much of the information your checklist requests,

  ▪ only your checklists promote <u>and protect your interests</u> with a set of questions from <u>your side </u>of the relationship,

  ▪ only your checklists equip you with questions that <u>apply specifically</u> to the decisions and actions of your financial advisor,

  ▪ only your checklists help you evaluate the <u>intent</u> of your financial advisor, and the <u>quality and professionalism</u> of your advisor, by how your questions are answered,

  ▪ only your checklists allow you to <u>record and file</u> your financial advisor's direct responses to your questions.

☐ The checklist questions are based on industry "best practices" for disclosure. There are no "zinger" or "gotcha" questions.

☐ Beware of evasive answers or claims that it's "against company policy" to answer.

After completion:

☐ Review for accuracy and completeness with your financial advisor.

☐ File the completed checklist in your *My Best Interests* folder.

What to Know

You probably know what you pay for most goods and services, but do you really know what you're paying in fees and other costs? <u>Excessive fees and other costs are money out of your pocket!</u> This can add-up to a lot of money over a several-year period. You could be paying out hundreds or even thousands of dollars every year that you'd scream about paying, if you knew.

Your Financial Advisor

Caution: Do not evaluate your advisor by cost alone. The value of sound guidance and stewardship within a trust-based relationship is difficult to price. But while guidance and stewardship are important, they can't be evaluated in isolation. The full context of the relationship must be taken into consideration. This includes the investment management skill and the cost containment efforts of your financial advisor.

The advisory fee for most fee-based accounts with larger financial institutions is typically set as a percentage of assets under management. Fees are typically charged on a quarterly basis. Some advisers deduct charges at the beginning of the quarter, and others deduct fees at the end of the quarter. Other payment methods include a flat fee, hourly rate, and a monthly retainer.

Many advisers offer what are generically referred to as a mutual fund "wrap" account. These accounts have two layers of fees: the fee you pay to your adviser, and the internal expenses of the mutual funds in your account. If, for example, the advisory fee is 1.25% annually and the average dollar-weighted expense ratio of the mutual funds in your account is 0.50%, then the total annualized fee you are paying is 1.75%. Refer to Quick Course: *Calculating Total Costs*, p. 133, for more information.

<u>Your adviser is required to re-confirm their advisory fee for managing your account on an annual basis.</u> In addition to this, you also want to know if there are investments in your account to which the fee does not apply, or should not apply. For example, if you have a limited partnership in your account, it may be difficult to justify paying the full advisory fee, or any fee, on that asset.

Your Financial Advisor

Having your advisor provide you with the total costs of doing business with them goes a long way in showing that you come first in the relationship, and that the trust and confidence you've placed in them is well-founded. Controlling your total costs is a good way to measure that.

The Checklist
The Importance of the Questions

Start the checklist by filling-in your account information and the reporting period.

1. **Your adviser will provide the following advisory fee information:**

   ☐ The advisory fee stated as either an annual percentage of assets, flat-fee, hourly rate, or monthly retainer.

   ☐ The full-year dollar amount you paid in advisory fees/rates.

   ☐ The dollar amount of any underlying expenses you paid in addition to the advisory fee. Note: These additional expenses may be in the form of internal expenses on mutual funds/ETFs, etc. If applicable, have your adviser use your account's period-closing investments and values.

   Note: These expenses aren't typically talked about or accounted for, but you pay them year after year. Calculating these costs is not difficult or time-consuming for your adviser to do. And while market conditions and additions/subtractions to holdings during the reporting period will affect the actual internal expenses you paid, it does provide a rough snapshot of your costs, while creating an awareness of them.

2. **Calculate your total costs.**

   You or your adviser will divide the total costs for the period by your account's closing value to get your total costs as a percentage of your account value.

? How do I know whether the checklist is completed properly?

Every field is filled and the total costs are calculated.

What do Advisory Services Generally Cost?

Most advisers charge an asset-based advisory fee stated as a percentage of the account value. The fee is generally higher for smaller accounts, and lower for larger accounts. For example, a $100,000 account may have an advisory fee between 1.25% and 1.75%. A $500,000 account may have an advisory fee between 1.00% and 1.50%. Accounts over $1 million generally have advisory fees below 1.00%. Your actual fee may be higher or lower than these examples.

If your adviser uses actively-managed mutual funds or separately managed accounts (SMA) through outside investment management firms to manage portions of your account, this is an expense you pay on top of your adviser's fee. This additional cost can range from 0.05% for indexed investments to over 1.00% for active management. If your adviser acts as the money manager of your account and invests only in individual stocks and bonds, you don't have this additional cost.

Whether it's commissions or advisory fees, the expense must have a business justification. For example, if your adviser provides exceptional ongoing advice and guidance, exceptional reporting and communication, and acts as an expert in providing you with other valuable services, 2.00% in total fees/costs may be justifiable and well worth it to you. If your advisor is simply camping on a mutual fund wrap fee, 1.00% may not be justifiable.

Some advisers charge an hourly rate for services. Many of these advisers focus more on financial planning than money management. Depending on the scope and complexity of your needs, hourly rates are generally between $100 and $300 an hour.

Total Costs: Fee-based Accounts
Dear advisor: just a few questions...

Date: _____

Title of account: _____

Firm: _____ Account number: _____

For the one-year reporting period: _____ to _____

Opening Account Value: $_____ Closing Value: $_____

Type of Advisory Fee:

      Asset-based advisory fee of _____% annually

      Flat-fee: $_____

      Hourly rate: $_____

      Monthly retainer rate: $_____

Full-year dollar amount paid in advisory fees/rates for the period: $_____

Estimated dollar amount paid during the reporting period in internal expenses on mutual funds/ETFs, etc. (if applicable) using period-closing investments and values*: $_____

                            Total Costs: $_____

Total Cost Calculation
Total estimated costs stated as a percentage of ending-period account value:

Total Costs $_____ / Closing Account Value $_____ = _____ %

Note: The Total Cost Calculation is best used to evaluate full-year costs.

* Calculating these costs is not difficult or time-consuming for your adviser to do. While market conditions and additions/ subtractions to holdings during the reporting period will affect the actual internal expenses you paid, it does provide a rough estimate of what you may be paying in internal expenses on mutual funds, ETFs and other products in your account.

Investment Scams and Fraud

Too Good to be True?

Checklist

Investment Scams and Fraud   p. 121

How Long Does it Take to Do?

About 5 minutes

When to Use

☐ Whenever you're being solicited to put money into a new investment program, product, scheme or other business opportunity that sounds "too good to be true".

BEING SCAMMED COULD HAVE LIFE-ALTERING CONSEQUENCES

Note: Photocopy the checklist before using.

Investment Scams and Fraud
Is this right for me, or too good to be true?

Instructions

Who completes the checklist?
You do. It's a phone call.

What to Know

We've all heard about investment scams and fraud. And most of us think: "that couldn't happen to me" or, "I'd never fall for that", but it does, and we do. Here's the statistics: the typical victim of investment scams and fraud are individuals 45 to 70 years-old. Most of these victims are financially literate and educated. Most have above-average incomes, and are generally inquisitive and confident.

Fraudsters typically approach their targets either directly, individual-by-individual, through referrals, or through affinity groups such as clubs, associations, or places of worship. Affinity group scams are successful because of the potential for peer influence and the false belief that if other people are investing, it must be okay.

Scam artists are good! They have highly-developed skills for communication and persuasion. Couple that with a friendly and disarming personality, and you may just "fall for it." Scam artists use several tactics. One example is persistency. Whether subtle or high-pressure, they literally wear you down – without you even realizing it. Creating scarcity and the need for immediacy is another tactic.

Scam artists try to get to know you personally. In doing so, they identify your strengths, your weakness, and where you're vulnerable. Another tactic is tried-and-true: sweet persuasion. With your good judgment suspended and your defenses down, you "fall for it." It's common for victims of fraud to comment after the fact: "I still can't believe it. I thought they were my friend." How do you protect yourself from investment scams and fraud? Be W.I.S.E:

Wait. Don't allow yourself to be hurried or bullied into making a decision.

Investigate the investment opportunity and the person pitching the offer. All investments are required by law to be registered with the state. That goes for the person making the pitch, too. And in most cases of fraud, neither is. So contact your state's securities regulator to confirm that the investment and the person making the sales pitch are registered.

Seek independent and expert third-party advice. Have a licensed financial advisor, attorney or accountant review the investment opportunity. Most of the money lost to scams and fraud is just that: lost; and often difficult to recover from both financially, and emotionally.

Educate yourself. Be suspicious of any opportunity that "sounds too good to be true."

Also, beware of common red-flag statements, like "guaranteed returns", "double your money", "cant' miss opportunity", "you must act now!"

We're all potential victims of investment fraud and scams. The skills of the criminal are not used to sell the features and benefits of a bogus investment. The investment is only a prop. Their skills are used for one purpose: to get you to turn over your money. They do this by disarming you and lulling you out of your natural skepticism and better judgment. And when that occurs, any one of us could "fall for it."

Investment Scams and Fraud
Investment programs, products, schemes and other business opportunities

Name of investment opportunity: _____

Name of salesperson: _____

1. Find contact information for your state's securities regulator. You can do this by visiting the North American Securities Administrators Association website at www.nasaa.org.

2. Call your regulator and provide information about the investment opportunity. They will confirm that the investment program, product, or scheme is licensed and registered, and that the salesperson is also licensed and registered.

3. If your regulators can't confirm that the investment opportunity and the salesperson are properly licensed and registered, *do not invest!*

☐ The investment product/opportunity is licensed and registered with my state's securities/insurance regulators. (Check the box)

Confirmed by me.   Date: _____

☐ The solicitor/salesperson is registered and licensed with my state's securities/insurance regulators. (Check the box)

Confirmed by me.   Date: _____

Quick Courses
Additional information without the fluff

Asset Allocation p. 123
Asset allocation is the starting point of the investment process. It is the process of divvying-up (allocating) your money among some - or all - of the asset classes of stocks, bonds, cash and other assets classes such as real estate, natural resources and precious metals. This course provides example allocations and general guidelines for allocating your money based upon your goal time horizon, the purpose of your account and its investment objective.

Investment Examples Categorized by Goal Time Horizon p. 125
Based on the time horizon of your investment-related goal, certain types of investments may generally be considered more appropriate than others. For example, if you have shorter-term, "must have money available" goals, then you might consider owning investments that are less likely to lose the money you'll need soon. If you have longer-term goals that require growth in the value of your money, you might consider owning investments that are more likely to make you money you'll need later. This course provides investment examples you can use as general guidelines.

Calculating Returns p. 127
If you're a 'do-it-yourselfer' or if you're just curious, this resource provides a quick-and-easy method for calculating the return on your account. With simple addition, subtraction, division and multiplication, returns can be calculated using information right from your brokerage account statement(s).

Benchmarking Returns p. 129
When performance is measured, performance improves. If you're a 'do-it-yourselfer' or if you're just curious, this resource provides you with an easy way to compare the return on your account against a single benchmark, or a blend of benchmarks, that accurately represent how the investments in your account are allocated. This course shows you generally-accepted ways to compare the return of an investment, or a whole account, against a benchmark.

Calculating Total Costs p. 133
In general, the "cost of doing business" with your financial advisor falls into three general categories: commissions/ advisory fees, front-end sales charges on mutual funds and other packaged investments, and the internal expenses you pay on mutual funds/exchange traded funds or ETFs. These costs can add up, especially over multiple-year periods. This course shows you how to calculate the total cost of doing business with your financial advisor.

Your Account Documents p. 136
This guide provides an overview of some of the more important documents and official communications associated with your brokerage account, including your new account form, trade confirmations and account statements. To promote and protect your best interests, you need to understand the purpose of these documents, and know how to read and interpret the information they contain.

Asset Allocation

Asset allocation is the starting point of the investment process. It is the process of divvying-up (or allocating) your money among some - or all - of the asset classes of stocks, bonds, cash and other secondary assets classes such as real estate, natural resources and precious metals. Most of the return pattern of your account is attributable to its asset allocation.

Having an asset allocation that is inconsistent with your investment objective, time horizon and your risk tolerance may have negative consequences. For example, having most of your account in less-risky fixed income investments when your risk tolerance and time horizon suggest having more in riskier growth investments, may result in lower returns and lost growth opportunity. Another example is having most of your account in riskier growth investments when your risk tolerance and investment time horizon suggest having more in less-risky fixed income investments. This may result in volatility that is higher than what you're willing to tolerate, and could also result in losses if you were to panic and sell.

The 'right' asset allocation for you is one that takes into consideration your investment objective, time horizon and how much risk you're willing to assume.

The following example allocations are general guidelines for allocating your money based upon your investment objective, time horizon and risk tolerance:

'Extremely-low risk' Allocation
Example allocation: 100% cash and cash equivalents
- ☐ CDs
- ☐ Savings
- ☐ Money market mutual funds
- ☐ Treasury bills

This allocation may generally be considered more appropriate for:
- ☐ Investment time horizons less than 3 years
- ☐ An investment objective that has no tolerance for risk
- ☐ Example investment objective: "Preservation of Principal"

'Lower-risk' Allocation
Example allocation range: 30% to 40% 'riskier' growth assets[1]

- ☐ Greater percentage allocated to bonds and cash than to riskier growth assets like stocks.

- ☐ Potentially more volatile than a portfolio with no allocation to growth assets such as stocks[2].

- ☐ Returns are generally derived from interest income rather than from dividends and capital appreciation, especially with higher percentage allocations to bonds and cash.

This allocation may generally be considered more appropriate for:
- ☐ Investment time horizons between 3 years and 5 years[3]
- ☐ An investment objective with a lower tolerance for risk
- ☐ Example investment objective: "Conservative Growth and Income"

'Moderate-risk' Allocation

Example allocation range: 40% to 60% 'riskier' growth assets

☐ An equal or slightly higher percentage allocated to riskier growth assets such as stocks than to bonds and cash.

☐ Potentially more volatile than a portfolio with a lower percentage allocation to riskier growth assets.

☐ Returns are generally derived from a mixture of dividends, interest income and capital appreciation.

This allocation may generally be considered more appropriate for:
☐ Investment time horizons between 6 years and 10 years[3]
☐ An investment objective with moderate tolerance for risk
☐ Example investment objective: "Moderate Growth and Income"

'Higher-risk' Allocation

Example allocation range: > 60% 'riskier' growth assets

☐ Higher percentage allocated to growth assets such as stocks than to bonds and cash.

☐ Potentially more volatile than a portfolio with a lower percentage allocation to riskier growth assets.

☐ Returns are generally derived from capital appreciation rather than from dividends and interest income, especially with higher-percentage allocations to stocks or other 'riskier' assets.

This allocation may generally be considered more appropriate for:
☐ Investment time horizons over 10 years
☐ An investment objective with a higher tolerance for risk
☐ Example investment objective: "Long Term Growth"

[1] For example real estate, hard assets e.g., gold and silver, and natural resources.

[2] Prices of bond mutual funds and ETFs fluctuate in value in response to movement in interest rates and bond credit ratings. In general, when interest rates decline, the prices of existing bonds rise in value. Conversely and in general, when interest rates rise, the prices of existing bonds decline in value. In general, the longer the maturity date, the more the bond is affected by movements in interest rates and bond credit ratings.

[3] For investment time horizons between 3 and 5 years, it may be appropriate to allocate a portion of your funds to stocks and other growth assets depending upon your investment objective and your willingness to assume the potential risk of a multiple-year period of negative stock returns. Historically, the potential risk of a negative return on stocks for a full holding period is greater for holding periods between 3 years and 5 years than it is for holding periods between 6 years and 10 years.

Disclaimer

The above asset allocation examples are provided for informational purposes only and do not constitute investment advice. There is no guarantee that any asset allocation example illustrated herein will achieve its objective, generate profits or avoid losses. Diversification does not guarantee investment returns and does not eliminate the risk of significant loss.

Example Investments Categorized by Goal Time Horizon

Based on the time horizon of your investment-related goal, certain types of investments may generally be considered more appropriate than others. For example, if you have shorter-term "must have money available" goals, then you might consider owning investments that are less likely to lose the money you'll need soon. If you have longer-term goals that require growth in the value of your money, you might consider owning investments that are more likely to make you money you'll need later. Longer-term investments that offer growth potential may not be appropriate for short-term timeframes because their potential for extreme volatility over the short-term may result in a loss of principal, if sold. Conversely, shorter-term investments that preserve the value of your money may not be appropriate for longer-term timeframes where 'growth' is the investment objective.

Shorter-term goals: < 3 years
Investment examples:

Cash equivalents

- [ ] U.S. Treasury Bills
- [ ] Bank or credit union savings accounts
- [ ] Stable value funds and money market funds
- [ ] CDs maturing < 3 years

Bonds

- [ ] Short-term individual bonds maturing < 3 years
- [ ] Target date maturity ETFs
- [ ] Short-term bond mutual funds and ETFs with average effective maturities < 3 years[1,2]

Intermediate-term goals: >3 years to 10 years
For intermediate-term timeframes, it may be appropriate to allocate a portion of your funds to stocks and other growth assets depending upon your investment objective and your willingness to assume the potential risk of a multiple-year period of negative stock returns. Historically, the potential risk of a negative return on stocks for a full holding period is greater for holding periods between 1 year and 5 years than it is for holding periods between 6 years and 10 years.

Investment examples:

Cash equivalents

- [ ] U.S. Treasury Bills
- [ ] Bank or credit union savings accounts
- [ ] Stable value funds and money market funds

Bonds (and other 'fixed-income' investments)

- [ ] CDs with maturity dates between 3 and 10 years
- [ ] Individual bonds with maturity dates between 3 and 10 years
- [ ] Target date maturity bond ETFs
- [ ] Intermediate-term bond mutual funds and ETFs with average effective maturities between 3 and 10 years[1, 2]

Stocks (and other 'growth' investments)

- ☐ Individual common stocks
- ☐ Stock mutual funds, closed-end stock funds (CEF), stock unit investment trusts (UIT), stock ETFs and 'Target Date' funds
- ☐ Real estate funds, hard asset (precious metals) funds, natural resources funds

Longer-term goals: >10 years

For longer-term timeframes, it may be appropriate to allocate a portion if not most of your funds to stocks and other growth assets depending upon your investment objective and your willingness to assume the potential risk of a multiple-year period of negative stock returns. Historically, the potential risk of a negative return on stocks for a full holding period is less for holding periods greater than 10 years than it is for holding periods between 6 years and 10 years.

Investment examples:

Bonds

- ☐ Target date maturity bond ETFs
- ☐ Longer-term individual bonds
- ☐ Long-term bond mutual funds and ETFs with average effective maturities >10 years [1,2]

Stocks (and other 'growth' investments)

- ☐ Individual common stocks
- ☐ Stock mutual funds, closed-end stock funds (CEF), stock unit investment trust (UIT), stock ETFs and 'Target Date' Funds
- ☐ Real estate funds, hard asset funds, natural resources funds

[1] Average effective maturity is a weighted average of all the maturities of the bonds in a mutual fund or exchange traded fund. It is calculated by weighting each bond's effective maturity by the market value of the security. Information on the average effective maturity of a bond mutual fund or ETF is available through your employer-sponsored retirement plan provider (for investments offered within the plan), mutual fund fact sheets, mutual fund company websites and mutual fund/ETF rating and ranking services.

[2] Prices of bond mutual funds and ETFs fluctuate in value in response to movement in interest rates and bond credit ratings. Unlike individual bonds, bond mutual funds and ETFs do not have a maturity date. They maintain an average maturity in accordance with their investment objective. For example, a short-term bond fund may maintain a constant average effective maturity of 2.5 years in perpetuity. Consequently, the value of your bond fund and/or ETF may be worth less than your original investment upon liquidation.

A quick-and-easy method for calculating the return on your account is the approximation method. With simple addition, subtraction, division and multiplication, returns can be calculated using information right from your brokerage account statement(s).

This method compares the account's ending value with its beginning value for the period, typically quarterly or annually, then adjusts for any additions or withdrawals. To keep this simple, there's a little fudging in how additions and withdrawals are accounted for: 50% of net additions/withdrawals are subtracted from the account's ending value and 50% of net additions/withdrawals are added to the account's beginning value. This creates a mid-period average for cash flows. If deposits and withdrawals are infrequent and not too sizeable, the approximation method provides a fairly accurate estimate of your return without any complicated calculations. Here's the formula:

$$\left(\frac{\text{Ending Value} - 0.50 \text{ Net Additions/Withdrawals}}{\text{Beginning Value} + 0.50 \text{ Net Additions/Withdrawals}} - 1.00 \right) \times 100 = \text{Return \%}$$

Example 1:

Ending period value: $100,000
Additions: $7,000
Withdrawals: $2,000
Beginning period value; $90,000

In this example, net additions into the account were $5,000. 50% of $5,000 is $2,500.

$$\left(\frac{100,000 - 2,500 = 97,500}{90,000 + 2,500 = 92,500} - 1.00 \right) \times 100 = \text{Return \%}$$

$$\frac{97,500}{92,500} = 1.054 - 1.00 = .054 \times 100 = 5.4\% \text{ Return}$$

Example 2:

If you have no additions or withdrawals from your account for the period, simply divide the ending period value by the beginning period value.

$$\frac{100,000}{90,000} = 1.111 - 1.00 = .111 \times 100 = 11.1\% \text{ Return}$$

While the beginning and ending values in example 1 and 2 were the same, additions and withdrawals affected the rate of return in example 1. The following overview of two popular methods for calculating returns will help explain why:

Dollar Weighted Rate of Return

This method measures the return on your invested dollars. It takes into account the beginning period account value, the ending period account value, and the date and amount of each addition or withdrawal. This method is also referred to as an internal rate of return. It shows returns you can "take to the bank". This method should be used when you want to compare your account's return against your goal-based return objective.

Time Weighted Rate of Return

This method assumes a *one dollar* investment at the beginning of a given time period and measures the growth of that dollar as a percentage rate of return, thus the term "time weighted". This method should be used to compare your account's return against the return of an index/benchmark like the S&P 500 index for example, or the return of a particular mutual or investment category against a benchmark or peer group (which also calculate returns assuming a one dollar investment at the beginning of a given time period.)

Your financial advisor welcomes the opportunity to explain the method they use to calculate the return on your account.

When performance is measured and compared, performance improves

To be in-the-know and in control over your investments, you need to have answers to two important questions about your account: "how is it doing?" and "compared to what?"

This module provides you with an easy way to compare the return on your account against a benchmark that accurately represents how the investments in your account are allocated. This method uses time-weighted returns, which are generally used for comparing the return of an investment, or a whole account, against a benchmark.

While other, more accurate (and more complicated) methods for measuring performance exist, the 11-step process used in this module is easy to follow and easy to do. Using only simple addition, subtraction and multiplication, you'll arrive at a "close enough" comparison between the return on your account and the return on a representative benchmark. First, some definitions are in order:

Index

An index is a method of measuring the value of a financial market e.g., the stock market or the bond market. An index can represent a broad market such as the S&P 500 Stock Index or the Barclays Capital US Aggregate Bond Index, or segments of a broad market such as the Dow Jones US Technology Index. Indices can also represent the market of a region, for example the MSCI European, Australasian, and Far Eastern (EAFE) Index or of a nation, for example the British FTSE 100. There are thousands of indexes. Some of the more popular ones are the S&P 500, the Dow Jones Industrial, and the NASDAQ 100.

Benchmark

A benchmark is a standard against which the performance of a security, mutual fund or broker/adviser can be measured. Generally, an index or an index mutual fund/ETF (exchange traded fund) is used as a benchmark. The objective of actively-managed mutual funds is to out-perform a representative benchmark, net of fees, when measured over a multiple-year period. Note: An index is a mathematical construct. You cannot invest directly in an index.

Let's get started

1. Select the measurement period e.g., quarter-to-quarter, end-of year.

To get started, select the reporting period you want to use. As a practical matter, use your most recent quarter-end or year-end statement.

2. Categorize the individual investments within your account by asset class.

Look at each investment in your account and determine whether it's composed mostly of stocks, bonds, cash or other asset classes such as real estate or natural resources. Your brokerage account/retirement plan account statement typically categorizes your investments this way.

Other sources include:

- ☐ Your employer-sponsored retirement plan provider (for investments you own within the retirement plan)
- ☐ Mutual fund prospectuses / fact sheets
- ☐ Mutual fund/ETF company websites
- ☐ Mutual fund/ETF rating and ranking services
- ☐ Financial/investment-related websites

Categorization example:

Asset Class: Stocks
ABC Large Cap Growth Fund
XYZ Large Cap Value Fund
DEF Small Cap Fund

Asset Class: Bonds
ABC Corporate Bond Fund
XYZ U.S. Government Bond Fund

3. List the beginning period value of each investment within each asset class. For example:

Asset Class: Stocks	Beginning Value
ABC Large Cap Growth Fund	$20,000
XYZ Large Cap Value Fund	$20,000
DEF Small Cap Fund	$20,000
Total Stocks	$60,000

Asset Class: Bonds	Beginning Value
ABC Corporate Bond Fund	$20,000
XYZ U.S. Government Bond Fund	$20,000
Total Bonds	$40,000

4. Calculate the percentage each investment represents of the total account value. You do this by dividing the dollar value of the investment by the account value. For example:

Beginning Period Account Value: $100,000

Asset Class: Stocks	Beginning Value	% of Account
ABC Large Cap Growth Fund	$20,000	20%
XYZ Large Cap Value Fund	$20,000	20%
DEF Small Cap Fund	$20,000	20%
Total Stocks	$60,000	60%

Asset Class: Bonds	Beginning Value	% of Account
ABC Corporate Bond Fund	$20,000	20%
XYZ U.S. Government Bond Fund	$20,000	20%
Total Bonds	$40,000	40%

Total Account Value	$100,000	100%

5. Next, get the published return of each investment for the period being measured. This information is available from:

☐ Your employer-sponsored retirement plan provider (for investments you own within the retirement plan)
☐ Mutual fund prospectuses / fact sheets
☐ Mutual fund/ETF company websites
☐ Mutual fund/ETF rating and ranking services
☐ Financial/investment-related websites

For example:

Investment	Return
ABC Large Cap Growth Fund	11%
XYZ Large Cap Value Fund	10%
DEF Small Cap Fund	12%
ABC Corporate Bond Fund	4%
XYZ U.S. Government Bond Fund	2%

6. Then calculate the 'weighted return value' for each investment. You do this by multiplying the investment's percentage weighting in the account by its return. For example:

Investment	Return	Weighted Return Value
ABC Large Cap Growth Fund	11%	20 X 1.11 = 22.2
XYZ Large Cap Value Fund	10%	20 X 1.10 = 22.0
DEF Small Cap Fund	12%	20 X 1.12 = 22.4
ABC Corporate Bond Fund	4%	20 X 1.04 = 20.8
XYZ U.S. Government Bond Fund	2%	20 X 1.02 = 20.4

7. Add-up the weighted return values.

Investment	Return	Weighted Return Value
ABC Large Cap Growth Fund	11%	20 X 1.11 = 22.2
XYZ Large Cap Value Fund	10%	20 X 1.10 = 22.0
DEF Small Cap Fund	12%	20 X 1.12 = 22.4
ABC Corporate Bond Fund	4%	20 X 1.04 = 20.8
XYZ U.S. Government Bond Fund	2%	20 X 1.02 = 20.4
Account Overall Return		107.8

8. Next, subtract 100 from the total. In this example, the overall return on the account was 7.8%.

Knowing the return is important, but by itself it isn't really helpful. It doesn't tell you whether the return was competitive or underperforming based on how your investments were allocated. To determine this, the return needs to be measured against a representative benchmark. How do you do this?

9. Get the representative benchmark for each investment. This information is also available through:

☐ Your employer-sponsored retirement plan provider
☐ Mutual fund prospectuses / fact sheets
☐ Mutual fund/ETF company websites
☐ Mutual fund/ETF rating and ranking services
☐ Financial/investment-related websites

Applied to the example account, a representative blended benchmark might be:

Account Asset Allocation	Blended Benchmark Example
40% Large Cap Stock Funds	40% S&P 500 Index
20% Small Cap Fund	20% Russell 2000 [Small Cap] Index
40% Bond Funds	30% BarCap U.S. Aggregate Bond Index

10. Next, get the published return for each benchmark for the period being measured. Then calculate the 'weighted return value' for each benchmark. Then add-up the weighted return values. For example:

Blended Benchmark Example	Return	Wtd. Return Value
40% S&P 500 Index	11%	40 X 1.11 = 44.4
20% Russell 2000 [Small Cap] Index	10%	20 X 1.10 = 22.0
30% BarCap U.S. Aggregate Bond Index	2%	40 X 1.02 = 40.8
Benchmark Return		107.2

Next, subtract 100 from the total. In this example, the benchmark return was 7.2%.

11. Compare the return of the account to its benchmark:

Portfolio Return	7.8%
Benchmark Return	7.2%

In this example, the account out-performed its benchmark by 0.6% for the measurement period.

Measuring your account return against a benchmark lets you know what's working, what's not working, and provides direction for addressing underperformance. For example, you can analyze each investment against its benchmark:

Investment	Return	Benchmark	Return
DEF Small Cap Fund	12%	Russell 200 Index	10%

You can also analyze an investment category against its benchmark. For example:

Investment	Return	Benchmark	Return
ABC Large Cap Growth Fund	11%	S& P 500 Index	11%
XYZ Large Cap Value Fund	10%		

Investment	Return	Benchmark	Return
ABC Corporate Bond Fund	4%	BarCap U.S. Agg. Index	2%
XYZ U.S. Government Bond Fund	2%		

Calculate the return on your account(s) at least annually.

Note: Gaining in popularity among brokers/advisers is goals-based investing. This approach manages your account to your financial goals and measures its return against a goals-based 'bogey' instead of against an external, index-based benchmark like the S&P 500 Index, for example. The argument is that the most important context is you and your goals - not the financial marketplace, and that meeting your financial goals is more important than beating the markets. In this context, "good performance" is a return that meets or beats your target return and keeps you moving ahead toward your goals, while "poor performance" is a return that has you falling behind. While measuring returns in the context of your goals may be the central consideration, it should not replace measuring returns against an external benchmark. Moving closer to goals while lagging behind an external benchmark is trouble. Falling behind on your goals-based benchmark while under-performing an external benchmark is double trouble.

Calculating Total Costs

In general, for most brokerage and advisory accounts the ongoing "cost of doing business" falls into four general categories:

- ☐ Commissions, mark-up/downs on stock and bond transactions
- ☐ Front-end sales charges on mutual funds and other 'packaged' products
- ☐ Advisory fees paid to your adviser
- ☐ Expenses on mutual funds/exchange traded funds or ETFs

In all probability, your costs come from more than one category. Some definitions are in order:

Commission
A service charge for buying or selling a security. For example a stock or ETF.

Markup
Certain securities, for example bonds, are available for purchase by retail investors from dealers who sell the securities directly from their own accounts. The markup is the difference between the price the security was purchased at and the price the dealer charges the retail investor.

Markdown
The amount subtracted from the selling price of a security. For example, a bond.

Front-end Sales Charge
The sales charge on a mutual fund is the difference between the price you pay per share for the fund and the fund's net asset value per share, or liquidation price.

Advisory Fee
What you pay your adviser for ongoing advice. Fees are generally calculated as a percentage of your account's assets, a flat fee or an hourly rate.

Expense Ratio
The expense ratio is the total percentage of mutual funds/ETFs assets used for advertising (12b-1), administrative, management, and all other expenses such as recordkeeping, custodial services and legal expenses. An expense ratio of 1% per annum means that each year 1% of the fund's total assets will be used to cover expenses. Translated to a dollar amount, a $25,000 mutual fund investment with a 1% expense ratio is $250 annually. Since fund performance is calculated net of expenses, expense ratios have a material effect on fund performance.

The expense ratio does not include the fund's trading activity, sales load or brokerage commissions. For more information on fund expenses and calculating fund expenses, visit FINRA Fund Analyzer at http://apps.finra.org/fundanalyzer/1/fa.aspx.

Commission-based Accounts

Commissions, Mark-up/downs

Calculate what the total cost in commissions and bond 'mark-up/mark-downs' represent as a percentage of the assets in your account for the period.

For example:
Beginning account value: $100,000
Period: full year

Transaction Type	Amount
Commissions	$1,000
Mark-up/mark-down	$250
	$1,250

In this example, the commissions and mark-up/down total $1,250. Stated as a percentage of the account's beginning value, this equals 1.25%.

Mutual Fund/ETF Expenses

Let's assume you have three mutual funds in your brokerage account and would like an estimate of what you're paying on an annual basis in fund expenses. The calculation is easy. For example:

Investment	Dollar Value	Expense Ratio %	Est. Annual Dollar Amount
Mutual Fund A	$50,000	1.25%	$625
Mutual Fund B	$25,000	0.95%	$238
ETF C	$25,000	0.15%	$38
	$100,000		$901

$901 \div 100,000 = 0.9\%$

Using ending period fund values and assuming no additions/withdrawals and no increase or decrease in the value of the funds, this calculation provides a rough estimation of what you might be paying on an annualized basis for your funds. In this example, the average weighted expense ratio for the funds you own is 0.9% or $901 annually.

Getting at Your Total Costs

For a complete accounting of what you're paying for and how much that is, include a rough estimation of any mutual fund/ETF expenses in the calculation. For example:

Beginning account value: $100,000
Period: full year

Transaction Type	Amount
Commissions	$1,000
Mark-up/mark-down	$250
Est. fund expenses (annualized)	$238
	$1,488

In this example, the commissions and mark-up/down total $1,250. The mutual fund has an estimated additional expense of $288 for a total of $1,488. Stated as a percentage of the account's beginning value, the total cost of doing business equals 1.49%.

Fee-based Accounts

Many fee-based advisers offer what are generically referred to as a mutual fund "wrap" account. With this type of account the adviser may either select a "model" portfolios (a preset allocation of mutual funds) that is appropriate for the purpose of your account, your investment objective, and tolerance for risk, or they may develop a customized portfolio for you based upon the same information. Then pre-screened mutual funds that meet certain criteria are selected for your portfolio. The adviser monitors the mutual funds and provides periodic performance reports. The expense ratios of these mutual funds add another level of fees.

If you have a mutual fund wrap account, calculate the average dollar-weighted expense ratio you're paying for the mutual funds in the portfolio. It's easy to calculate. For example:

Investment	Dollar Value	Expense Ratio %	Est. Annual Dollar Amount
Mutual Fund A	$20,000	0.60%	$120
Mutual Fund B	$20,000	0.50%	$100
Mutual Fund C	$20,000	1.15%	$230
ETF E	$20,000	0.10%	$20
ETF F	$20,000	0.15%	$30
	$100,000		$500

$500 \div 100,000 = 0.50\%$

Using ending period fund values and assuming no additions/withdrawals and no increase or decrease in the value of the funds, the calculation will provide you with a rough estimation of what you might be paying on an annualized basis for the funds in your portfolio. This amount is in addition to the fee you're paying to your adviser.

Getting at Your Total Costs

For a complete accounting of what you're paying for and how much that is, have your adviser calculate the total costs associated with your account. For example:

Beginning account value: $100,000
Period: full year

Fees/Expenses	Amount
Advisory fees	$1,250
Est. fund expenses (annualized)	$500
	$1,750

If, for example, your advisory fee is 1.25% annually and the average dollar-weighted expense ratio of the mutual funds in your account is 0.50%, then the total annualized fee you are paying is an acceptable 1.75%.

If you have a fee-based advisory account, you need to re-confirm on an annual basis, the fee you are paying. You also want to confirm if there are investments in your account to which the fee does not apply, or should not apply. For example, if you own a real estate, oil & gas or equipment leasing limited partnership within your advisory account, it may be difficult to justify paying the full advisory fee, or any fee, on those assets.

Your Account Documents: Boring but Important!

This guide provides an overview of some of the more important documents associated with your brokerage account: what to know, what to check, and what to look out for.

Your Investment Profile

When you open a brokerage account, your financial advisor gathers a lot of information about you. Much of this information is used to create an "investment profile" of you.

"Okay…
So why is my investment
profile important to me?"

It's used by your advisor to determine whether a particular recommendation or investment strategy is right for you. In regulatory-speak, "right" is called "suitability".

The "suitability standard of care" requires your advisor to "have a reasonable basis to believe" that a particular recommendation is suitable for you. Your investment profile helps with this."

So what information is included in your investment profile?

☐ Your investment experience.
This includes your level of knowledge on certain types of investments, and the number of years you've been investing in them.

☐ Your investment objective.
With the assistance of your advisor, you set your investment objective. Investment objectives are the marching orders for your account. Your advisor uses your account's investment objective along with information in your investment profile to determine what types of investments are suitable for you. But caution is in order:

No uniform definitions for investment objectives exist. So you must insist that your advisor carefully and fully explains what each investment objective means, and gives examples. Another cautionary note: incorrectly stating investment objectives at the firm level does occur. For example, you may be a "conservative" investor, but your investment objective is improperly stated as "aggressive". This has implications for "suitability" and in any disputes.

☐ Your risk tolerance.

As with investment objectives, uniform definitions do not exist. Since you set your risk tolerance, you must insist that your advisor carefully and fully explains what each risk tolerance definition means and gives examples. Many firms offer questionnaires to help you determine your risk tolerance.

☐ Your investment time horizon.
This refers to the length of time you have to meet your investment goal(s). <u>In addition to your risk tolerance, your investment time horizon is an important consideration when making investment recommendations.</u> Why? Because certain types of investments are generally considered more appropriate for shorter time horizons, and other types are considered more appropriate for longer time horizons.

☐ Liquidity needs.
For example if you need funds on a regular basis or have planned expenses that will require funds from your account, your advisor needs to know this.

Other information and "essential facts" about you that are required on your brokerage account application include:

☐ Your name
☐ Social Security number: Your firm uses your Social Security number for IRS reporting and to comply with the USA Patriot Act of 2001 to prevent terrorist financing and money laundering.
☐ Age: Your advisor photocopies your driver's license or passport to comply with the USA Patriot Act.
☐ Address
☐ Phone number
☐ Employment status
☐ Annual income
☐ Tax bracket (highest marginal rate)
☐ Net worth

Updating Your Account Information
Your financial advisor is required to periodically update your account information and investment profile.

" What if my financial or personal circumstances change?"

" It is your responsibility to inform your advisor in a timely manner. It may warrant a change in your account's investment objective and your risk tolerance."

Account Type: Cash and Margin
Knowing your account type is important. Most brokerage firms offer at least two types of accounts.

Cash Account
A "cash" account is generally coded as a Type 1 account and a "margin" account is typically coded as a Type 2 account. These codes are explained in the "Disclosures and Definitions" section of your statement. In a cash or Type 1 account you pay for your securities in full by the "settlement date" (generally three business days) either by depositing funds or with proceeds from the sale of securities.

Margin Account

In a margin loan account or Type 2 account, your brokerage firm can lend you funds to pay for the securities being purchased. The securities in your account serve as collateral for the loan. This is called buying securities "on margin." For example, if you purchase securities totaling $20,000 and you pay $10,000 and your brokerage firm lends you the other $10,000, the borrowed amount of $10,000 is your margin balance. Your brokerage firm charges interest on this balance. You are liable for the margin balance and the interest incurred. Most brokerage firms have minimum equity requirements of $5,000 to $10,000 for margin accounts.

 There are special risks with margin accounts that are not associated with cash accounts. Confirm with your financial advisor that your account type (Type 1 "cash" account or Type 2 "margin" account) is appropriate for you.

Trade Confirmations

Your brokerage firm is required to provide you with written communication for each brokerage transaction executed on your behalf. These official communications with you are referred to as "trade confirmations" or trade confirms. In addition to other information, confirms generally provide the following details about the trade:

☐ Whether the trade was solicited or unsolicited.

 The deliberate mismarking of solicited trades as unsolicited does occur. Unethical advisors do this to hide improper and unauthorized trades. Be sure you always check:

☐ Whether it was a buy or a sell
☐ Name of the security
☐ Quantity bought or sold
☐ Execution price
☐ Principal amount of the transaction
☐ Commission
Always check this. If it is not the agreed-upon amount or seems excessive, contact your advisor and request a corrected confirm.
☐ Any additional security description, information or required trade disclosures.

" That's a lot of information to review."

" Trade confirms are generally easy to read. It takes only a few seconds to review the information. Don't throw them in a pile and forget about them!"

Note

It is your responsibility to review your trade confirmations. If you find discrepancies or trades you believe may not have been authorized by you, contact your financial advisor immediately to discuss the matter.

Match-up your trade confirms with the Account Activity section of your account statement to make sure there are no errors. Keep your trade confirms in a paper or electronic folder. You'll use them to document gains and losses for tax purposes.

Trade Confirm Delivery Options

- ☐ Paper trade confirms are delivered by the US Postal System.
- ☐ Email: You receive an email alert that contains a hyperlink to a printable electronic image of the trade confirm on your firm's website.

Account Statement

Your brokerage account statement is the official document for complete information pertaining to your account's value, holdings, and activity. Knowing what information is in your statement helps you stay on top of what's going on in your account. While account statements can look different from firm to firm, they all have this information in common.

- ☐ Account information
- ☐ Account summary
- ☐ Income
- ☐ Fees
- ☐ Account activity
- ☐ Margin
- ☐ Portfolio detail
- ☐ Disclosures and definitions

Brokerage firms are required to provide you with a statement at least quarterly. If your account has frequent activity, you may receive monthly statements. As with bank accounts, most firms provide you with the option to receive your statement (and other account-related documents) either electronically or through the mail.

Special note: The brokerage firm you have your account with may not be the firm that generates your account statement. Your brokerage firm may be an "introducing" firm that takes orders from their customers and then "clear" or "settle" the trades through a "clearing" firm. Clearing firms finalize trades and hold the securities for the introducing firm. Typically it is the clearing firm that generates the account statement, not the introducing firm. <u>To reduce the potential of you being defrauded through forged statements, the Financial Industry Regulatory Authority or FINRA requires that all brokerage account statements contain the clearing firm's name and contact information.</u>

Account Information

The account information section shows:

- ☐ The statement reporting period
- ☐ Your account number
- ☐ Account type
- ☐ Titling on your account
- ☐ Your address of record
- ☐ Account investment objective (optional)

Investment Objective

Many brokerage account statements show the investment objective of the account, for example "Moderate Growth and Income" or "Long Term Growth". This information is important on two counts:

- [ ] It allows you to re-confirm your investment objective.
- [ ] You can confirm that the securities listed in the "Portfolio Detail" section are consistent with your investment objective and your financial advisor's investment strategy.

The account information section also shows:

- [ ] The name of your brokerage firm
- [ ] Your financial advisor's name
- [ ] Office address and phone number, and
- [ ] The clearing firm's name, address and phone number. (Required by FINRA)

Account Summary

The account summary section typically shows:

- [ ] Beginning account value for the period (month or quarter),
- [ ] Summary of account activity including cash deposits, cash withdrawals, dividends and interest, fees charged, and
- [ ] Closing account value for the period.

It may also include a pie chart and a tabular summary of your account's investments by asset class or investment type e.g., mutual funds or annuities, and the estimated annual income generated from your holdings. Complete information on the individual investments in your account is provided in the "Portfolio Detail" section.

Special note: While a summarization of the beginning and ending value of your account is a quick and convenient way to see whether your account was up or down for the period, it may not tell you whether the securities in the account contributed or detracted from the ending balance. A closing balance that is higher or lower than the opening balance may be the result of deposits or withdrawals, or from interest and dividend payments being credited to the account. The "Portfolio Detail" section of your statement provides the ending value for each investment and the total value by asset class or investment type in your account. You, or you with your advisor can review the investments and their values in this section and compare them with the previous period statement.

Account Activity

The categories of activity include:

- [ ] Credits and debits
- [ ] Interest and dividend income
- [ ] Charges and fees
- [ ] Transfers and journals
- [ ] Securities transactions

Many brokerage firms provide consolidated information on the account's income, credits and debits in the account summary section. As with a bank checking account, it is important for you to reconcile the flow of funds into, out of, and within your brokerage account.

It's important that you review the trading activity in your account and reconcile the transactions with the trade confirmations you receive. It's also important for you to confirm that the transactions, and the frequency of transactions, are appropriate for your account's investment objective. The guide *Trading Activity* will be helpful. If you have questions on specific trades or need further clarification, discuss the matter with your advisor. He or she welcomes every opportunity to help keep you informed and in-the-know about the activity in your account.

Portfolio Detail

This section provides a complete inventory of the individual investments in your account. The inventory includes the investment's name, ticker symbol or CUSIP, share quantity/number of bonds, cost basis (if available), current price, current market value (quantity x market price), estimated annual income and percentage yield.

Typically, brokerage firms categorize investments by asset class, e.g., stocks/ETFs, fixed-income and cash. Mutual funds are typically listed separately by asset class, e.g., stock mutual funds and bond mutual funds. Annuities and alternative investments are typically listed separately. A summarization of the "Portfolio Detail" section is typically provided in the "Account Summary" section in the form of a pie chart or table.

Disclosures and Definitions

This section helps you understand your statement by providing legal and administrative explanations about fees, penalties, and the terms and codes used in your statement. "Stuffers" and brochures (some mandated by regulators) may also be included in your account statement.

Consolidated Reports

Some advisors provide consolidated account reports to their customers. These reports combine the information of several accounts into one document. While consolidated reports are convenient, they do not replace your account statement which is the official document for complete information pertaining to your account's value, holdings, and activity.

 Carefully check the information in your consolidated report against each official account statement. The potential for inaccurate, confusing or misleading information exists.

It is your responsibility to check for inaccuracies or discrepancies in any of your statements. If they appear, contact your broker/adviser immediately.

Four things to do when you receive your statement:

☐ Confirm accuracy of account information including investment objective

☐ Know why your account increased or decreased in value from the previous reporting period. If you can't figure this out, talk to your financial advisor.

☐ Review account activity with special attention to fees and charges, deposits and withdrawals, transfers, journals and letters of authorization.

☐ Review trade activity.

Made in the USA
Charleston, SC
29 September 2015